4/40.

CRICKET REFLECTIONS
Five Decades of Cricket Photographs

KEN KELLY
CRICKET REFLECTIONS
Five Decades of Cricket Photographs

Text by David Lemmon
Foreword by Sir Leonard Hutton

PEERAGE BOOKS

To research a book covering nearly fifty years of cricket is quite a task, and to do it without help is impossible. I am indebted to many friends, colleagues and former cricketers for their valuable assistance; they gave me the chance to gather some of my earlier photographs from their personal albums and files. My thanks go to 'Tom' Dollery, Dick Spooner, Tom Pritchard, Judy Parkes and Reg Hayter.

Two newspaper offices let me search through their libraries for information and for my old photographs: I thank the management of *The Yorkshire Post* Newspapers Ltd (especially Irving Crawford, Photographic Manager, and Kathleen Rainford, Library). Thanks are also due to the management of *The Birmingham Post & Mail* Ltd (especially John Holland, Editor of *The Birmingham Post* and the *Evening Mail*, and Hazel Kennedy, Chief Librarian). Both also gave me permission to use certain photographs.

The Leeds Reference Library and Warwickshire County Cricket Club gave me access to their files.

A close friend and former *Yorkshire Evening News* colleague, Jack Hickes, found some old pictures and gave me permission to use them.

For over twenty years I worked with the old 'Long Tom' cameras; although little is known about this equipment, or the photographers who used it, many colleagues from that era have come to my assistance with information and photographs to enable the story to be written. My thanks go to Jack Hickes, Irving Crawford, Frank Carlill (Leeds and Birmingham), Dennis Oulds (Central Press), 'Ned' Evans (Press Association), Brian Thomas (former *Sport and General*), Geoff Hallawell (Manchester) and Bob Stiggins (*News Chronicle* and *Daily Express*). Other information was provided by Alex Bannister (formerly *Daily Mail*), with Patrick Eagar and David Frith giving help on the Australians.

The production of a book is a real team effort, and working with David & Charles has been a great experience. I give my thanks to all concerned, especially to Nigel Hollis (Editor) and Mike Head (Designer).

Statistics used have been taken from *Who's Who of Cricketers*, with additional information from Roy Wilkinson and Robert Brooke.

My friend David Lemmon has penned the text with his usual literary skill.

My sincere thanks go also to Graham Tarrant, who helped me to shape the book in its early stages, and who found a publisher; and to one of the cricketing greats, one of my early heroes, Sir Leonard Hutton, who has written the foreword. This brought back many memories, and has taken me right back to my Yorkshire roots.

Finally, to my wife Kate and daughters, Katherine and Susan: you gave me encouragement when I most needed it, and without you it would not have been possible.

KEN KELLY
May 1985

First published in Great Britain in 1985 by
David & Charles (Publishers) Limited

This edition published in 1989 by
Peerage Books
Michelin House
81 Fulham Road
London SW3 6RB

ISBN 1 85052 136 0

Produced by Mandarin Offset
Printed and bound in Hong Kong

Title page
Worcestershire *v* Australia, Worcester, 11 May 1985. Geoff Lawson is bowling to Tim Curtis, the Worcestershire opening batsman, who scored 76. The non-striking batsman is Phil Neale, who scored 108. This Worcestershire New Road ground is one of the most beautiful sights in cricket

Photographic Introduction

Each stage in the evolution of cricket photography has been inspired by the work of earlier photographers. It is then up to the next generation to consolidate, improvise and, if possible, to improve on these ideas. In this way progress and innovation is kept alive and becomes a continuous process; much of this story is told in a chapter at the end of this book.

These pictures are a photographic introduction to the book, which is essentially a cricket book, told through the medium of cricket photography. The pictures reproduced on this page span eighty-two years, during which time the photographic equipment, and the conditions in which the pictures are taken, have changed considerably.

Today, photographs are taken during the match, showing the action as it unfolds before the assembled crowd, as in the picture on the right. Dennis Lillee is shown leaping into his delivery stride; the picture was taken from some 90 yards away with an 800mm lens and on a 35mm format camera, during the England *v* Australia Test at Edgbaston in 1981.

The three photographs below were taken in 1899 by W. A. Rouch; he would have used a large format studio camera. The photographers of that time had a wicket marked out in a practice area and the player whether batsman or bowler was asked to go through his paces whilst the photographer took his pictures from a few yards away. The umpire did not, therefore, appear in the photograph.

The author noticed that these pictures of Sydney Santall, who played for Warwickshire between 1892 and 1914, were taken in the same location and would, when joined together, become a bowling sequence. The photographer, W. A. Rouch, took them as single action pictures and they were used that way in the books of that era; they are shown here as possibly the first ever bowling sequence pictures. Modern sequence pictures of bowlers are reproduced on pages 156 and 157, but with the innovation of the motor-wind it is a very much easier operation.

The photographs in the following pages cover nearly fifty years of cricket photography. They were taken in two distinct eras: that of the 'Long Tom' cameras, which were homemade, and that of 35mm equipment which is now sold in most camera shops and can be bought by anyone.

Foreword by Sir Leonard Hutton

Over a hundred years ago W. G. Grace predicted that the time would come when scores and reports of matches in Australia would be cabled to England. The first basic step in communications was duly taken, but the Grand Old Man would stroke his beard in awed amazement, if he returned today, at the miracle of television which brings the action, as it happens, to our armchairs from any part of the world.

I am sure he would heartily approve of the enormous strides in photography. Cricket in his day had to be content with 'mug' shots of head and shoulders, team photographs and stilted, posed studies of the foremost players demonstrating how to play forward, bowl an inswinger and so on. All very tame.

Now the drama and excitement are captured by highly sophisticated equipment and specialist cameramen who need to concentrate as hard as an opening batsman, and anticipate like a wicket-keeper.

Since the thirties, professionals of consummate skill such as the author of this record have greatly enriched cricket photography. It is now an art form. Ken Kelly needs to be both a technical expert of his craft and to have a highly developed knowledge of the game. Without an almost sixth sense it would be impossible for him to record an incident as it happens.

Mr Kelly has an excellent cricket pedigree starting with the advantage of being born in a house in Kirkstall Lane overlooking the Headingley ground where I was taught my trade by George Hirst. Ken saw every run of Sir Don Bradman's incredible aggregate of 963 in Test matches on the ground and, like a true Yorkshireman, he reels off the names and records of the county's legendary heroes from Herbert Sutcliffe onwards. Starting his career with the *Yorkshire Evening News*, he moved from Leeds to Birmingham where he has been based in recent years. But whenever a big match is being played Ken Kelly and his camera are a familiar sight.

David Lemmon is an excellent complementary writer for Ken Kelly and as the pros say every picture tells a story, and with this brilliant, patient labour of love Mr Kelly has made a striking contribution to cricket and cricket photography.

Len Hutton

The Headingley ground as it was just before and just after World War II

The old and the new – Ken Kelly with his last 'Long Tom' made for him in 1956 and with a 600mm lens bought in 1969 (*Picture by Rebecca Naden*)

Introduction

To be born in Yorkshire is to be born with cricket in the blood; to be born in a house in Kirkstall Lane overlooking the Headingley ground is to be born with cricket implanted permanently in the soul.

Ken Kelly's mother said that her son's first sight of the world was the view of Headingley Cricket Ground from the front bedroom window. Perhaps it was this sight, set so firmly in the subconscious, that has made Ken Kelly spend most of his life on cricket grounds throughout England and Australia, capturing for others the joys of the game and bequeathing a permanent record.

With only a few yards separating his home from the famous Test ground, Ken would dash home from school whenever there was cricket at Headingley. After four o'clock children were admitted for one penny, and for that sum you could watch the greatest cricketers in the world. In the 1930s Yorkshire breathed cricket and boasted a team which could win the County Championship seven times in nine years. They prided themselves, with ample justification, on being the best in the world.

Cheap though the entrance fee was for boys after four o'clock, it was not always easy to find a penny in those days and if a group of seven or eight wanted to watch the match, it was left to Ken to exploit one of the 'free' entrances that he knew so well, particularly at the rugby ground end. Once in the ground he would scout around for empty 'pop' bottles and take them to the bar or food counter where they would give a penny for the return of each bottle. When he had enough money he would go to the entrance gate and pay for his friends to come in legally. Once or twice he had to explain himself to the secretary, John Nash, who knew him as he had seen him bowling in the nets.

John Nash gave the young lad a dressing down and told him he would set stewards to guard the places where he crept into the ground. The secretary was rather put out when the boy told him he knew at least eleven, for there were not that many stewards to spare.

In the 1950s, when Ken Kelly was working for the *Birmingham Gazette*, he had to cover a match between Yorkshire and Warwickshire at Headingley and wrote to John Nash for a photographer's pass. Back came the reply: 'We seem to be out of photographers' passes at the moment. Can you gain entrance the same way that you used to as a boy?'

Great as was the White Rose side of the 1930s, it was an Australian who captured Yorkshire hearts in those years before World War II, and in spirit they made him an honorary Yorkshireman because he played cricket in the way that they understood.

Don Bradman played four Test matches at Headingley. In his first innings there in 1930 he scored 334. Four years later he made 304 and in 1938 he hit 103 and 16. His last Test there was in 1948 when Australia were set to make 404 on the last day on a turning wicket. Bradman had scored 33 in the first innings, but he followed it with 173 not out in the second as he and Arthur Morris put on 301 for the second wicket and took Australia to victory. This brought Bradman's aggregate to 963 runs in six innings at an average of 192.60 in his four Tests at Leeds, and Ken Kelly watched every run that he scored, first as a lad scarcely ten years old, then as a press photographer.

In 1948, Yorkshire County Cricket Club made Bradman an Honorary Life Member and presented him with a silver tray embossed in white enamel with the white rose of Yorkshire. Ken's adulation of Bradman as a cricketer and as a man has never diminished. He first approached Bradman as a photographer requesting pictures and was always treated with courtesy. Then, in January 1966, Mike Smith, the England captain, invited Ken Kelly onto the players' balcony during the third Test match at Sydney. The 'Don' was also on the balcony and Kelly was able to talk to him for a while. The hero grew in stature on closer acquaintance.

Ten years later Kelly shocked his journalist colleagues in Australia by announcing that he was going to take the long train journey from Melbourne to Sydney rather than make the short air trip. It was an act of homage. Kelly had stayed with a friend in Melbourne, Eric Wadsworth, a former colleague on the *Birmingham Gazette*, who, following a New Year party, put him on the train at Melbourne Central station early in the morning. The train stopped at Cootamundra and Ken Kelly walked on the platform for a while. It was his pilgrimage to Bradman's birthplace. A short time later the train passed through Bowral so that the homage to Bradman was complete.

Ken's passion for cricket, and Yorkshire cricket in particular, had come by birth; his career as a press photographer came almost by accident. It was easy to gravitate towards the cricket ground in spring and when net practice was being held, and once a youngster had plucked up courage to ask permission he was usually allowed to bowl to his idols, so that friendships were established with Leyland, Verity, Sutcliffe, Wood and the rest which flourished with the years.

Don Bradman, 1948 vintage

The Yorkshire team of 1936: Bright Heyhirst (masseur), Len Hutton, Hedley Verity, Bill Bowes, Frank Smailes, Cyril Turner, Arthur Wood, William Ringrose (scorer), Wilf Barber, Herbert Sutcliffe, Brian Sellers, Maurice Leyland, Arthur Mitchell

Ken Kelly's talents as an artist were recognised at Wyther Park Council School and he won a scholarship to Leeds College of Art where up to twenty places were offered each year. His main interests were lettering and commercial and industrial design. Indeed, he graduated from the college with the National Diploma of Design, but by then he had been gripped by his great passion for photography, inherited from an aunt who was a keen amateur photographer.

Equally great was his love for sport in general, and cricket in particular. Under the influence of his former art master at Wyther Park School, Maurice Carlton, a more than useful slow left-arm bowler, he played for Kirkstall Educational, a club to which Bill Bowes was attached, but the opportunities for playing were limited to weekends; during the summer months Ken Kelly watched as much cricket as possible and seemed lost when none was available.

One day he met Jack Slater, who was a friend of his father's and worked on the *Yorkshire Evening News*. Knowing that Ken was an art student with an interest in photography and that he was at a loose end, Slater suggested that he should meet John Hutchinson, the chief photographer of the newspaper.

The young art student was interviewed by Hutchinson and offered a job as photographic assistant for the rest of the summer. Two weeks later Ken Kelly was a member of the *Yorkshire Evening News* photographic team at Headingley for the fourth Test match between England and Australia. When he arrived at

the ground on 22 July 1938, he could not have anticipated that in thirty-five years' time he would be photographing his hundredth Test match. He had still not recovered from the shock that he was being paid to watch Bradman bat on the ground where he had seen him score 638 runs in two innings.

In 1938, cricket photography was still in its infancy and the two agencies, Central Press and Sport and General, were to hold the monopoly for another thirty-four years. Local newspapers, like the *Yorkshire Evening News*, were allowed to photograph at Headingley, but the two big agencies held firm national control. It is difficult for people today to realise quite how restrictive were the practices in sports coverage before World War II. Howard Marshall, one of the greatest of sports commentators, was not allowed to broadcast from Lord's at that time and some of his best summaries were given from a house in St John's Wood Road.

There was no specialist cricket camera equipment. It could be bought neither from a shop nor from a manufacturer. The enthusiast searched for a telephoto lens which, when found, would be housed in a lovingly designed and constructed mounting with a plate camera at the back. It was an object at which even the amateur photographer of today with his expensive and sophisticated equipment would shudder, but the 'Long Tom' cameras were made by craftsmen.

The 'Long Tom' was the name given to the lens, the housing and the camera. Nearly all the lenses before World War II had been made originally for aerial photography from balloons or zeppelins; and most had been made in Germany by Zeiss and others. The first equipment that Ken Kelly used at Headingley in 1938 had a Dallmeyer 40″ lens.

Ken's father, a director of a printing business, wished him to join the firm to work on design and layout for the colour brochures and booklets that they produced; but when he left college in 1939, he was offered a job on the permanent staff of the *Yorkshire Evening News*. Obsessed by sport and photography and seeing the chance of working with the newspaper as more exciting than sitting at a desk, he seized the opportunity. This was to be the last year of the great Yorkshire side, although none could have known that at the beginning of the season, however dark the clouds of Hitler loomed.

The cricket photographer needs three main qualities: skill, patience and a knowledge of the game. The young man from the *Yorkshire Evening News* had quickly acquired the first, helped in no small measure by his studies at Leeds College of Art where artistic vision and temperament were needed for understanding the composition of a picture, had soon learned the necessity of the second and had, in effect, been born with the third. He had bowled to the Yorkshire players in the nets from the time that he was thirteen and had grown closer to them. They respected his enthusiasm,

Johnny Muscroft (*Yorkshire Post*) and John Hutchinson (*Yorkshire Evening News*) using the 'Long Toms' from Headingley pavilion in 1938, England v Australia

his love for cricket and his sensitivity to the game, and the fact that he now attempted to record their endeavours for all to see strengthened a bond, for the relationship between photographer and his subject is a strong, if not unique one.

The cricket photographer is not always attempting to take pictures of perfectly executed shots so that he can publish a coaching manual; he is trying to record the incident, the character of the player and the humanity of the game. He is concerned with the essence of the sport which is character. No young photographer could have had a better grounding than one who was involved with Yorkshire cricket in the late 1930s, for no county has been richer in character than Yorkshire was at that time.

It was a time of class distinctions when amateurs and professionals changed in different dressing-rooms and came onto the field through different gates. In Yorkshire, Ken Kelly found that most of the 'players' were 'gentlemen' and certainly one of the amateurs, Brian Sellers, was very much a 'player'.

Sellers had become vice-captain of the side in 1932 and, as Greenwood, the appointed captain, was often unavailable, Sellers led the team twenty-five times and did not lose a match. Next season he became captain in his own right and a new era had begun.

As a batsman he was not really good enough for the side so he had to prove to older men, hardened professionals, that he, a young amateur, was suitable to lead them. He proved that point within a matter of weeks. He welded some great individual players into a team, a feat that was achieved with determination and discipline. He turned good fielders into great ones and all his men into good fielders. Above all, he treated the game, and the people who watched, with respect.

11

He made a century against the Australians at Bramall Lane in 1934 and he became the iron man of cricket, fearless as a fielder close to the wicket. Later he was to become a Test selector and he brought the same wisdom and dedication to that job that he had done to moulding his Yorkshire side and giving it its corporate character. Within the framework that was necessary for the success of the team individual personalities abounded and flourished.

First there was Herbert Sutcliffe, the senior professional, who, like Brian Sellers, gave every encouragement to young men like Ken Kelly. At a practice session he would put a sixpence, shilling or even a florin on top of his stumps, the prize for bowling him out. If one of the youngsters bowled well, or had simply given him a good net, he would miss the ball at the end of the session and allow the lad to win the money. He gave no such help to bowlers on the field. With his two famous opening partners, Hobbs for England and, initially, Holmes for Yorkshire, he had become part of cricket's folklore. Always immaculate, with his black hair brushed into a position from which it was never ruffled, his appearance revealed his character, calm and unflappable.

Sutcliffe was not a polished, elegant batsman, but temperamentally the world has seen no better player, an impeccable judge of length, pace and direction with courage, determination and concentration unparalleled. He played for Yorkshire for twenty years and he was, to Ken Kelly as to others, the 'gentleman-player'. There was a time when he came close to leading Yorkshire, an honour he declined in order to perpetuate the tradition of the amateur captain, for he was a man of tradition and honour. And the Yorkshire traditions he guarded most jealously were those of toughness, smartness and success. It is said that when he was hit he refused treatment, simply shouting down the pitch, 'We Sutcliffes do not feel pain.'

His self-possession and confidence could bring his opponents to the point of despair. He and Percy Holmes set up a world record opening stand of 555 against Essex at Leyton in 1932. Six years later Sutcliffe and Hutton had scored 315 before tea against Leicestershire at Hull, and as they went out to continue the stand after the interval the elder states-

Brian Sellers leads the Yorkshire team out at Bradford in 1939: Verity, Yardley, Mitchell, Wood and Sellers

man turned to the twenty-one-year-old Hutton and said, with complete sobriety, 'We'll go for 556.'

There is a scruffiness about today's players which would have been alien to Herbert Sutcliffe who always carried two bags, one the old-fashioned conventional cricket bag, the other a flat case in which flannels and shirts were kept, pressed and spotless. Kelly remembers that even when Sutcliffe walked into the Yorkshire grounds after the war, having long since stopped playing, he was always immaculate and was always recognised and applauded by the crowd.

Occasionally, Herbert Sutcliffe had as his opening partner Arthur 'Ticker' Mitchell. (The nickname had come from his habit of continuing to natter, or 'ticker-on', while play was in progress.) Mitchell was a fearsome character for a young player, let alone a budding photographer, to deal with for it was said of him that he had a career record of never having praised a colleague or an opponent, and when, after retirement, he became county coach, he guarded traditional Yorkshire values with an unrelenting severity.

Mitchell joined Yorkshire as a hard-hitting batsman, but he became so imbued with his interpretation of the dour county spirit that he tended to carry caution to extremes as his career progressed. He epitomised the accepted idea of the Yorkshire character.

It was said that, as a young player, he had fielded all day at Southampton when Wilfred Rhodes, having bowled almost non-stop, had not conceded a boundary. With only fifteen minutes to go to the end of play, Mitchell allowed a ball to go through his legs for 4, the first and only boundary of the day off Rhodes. Wilfred did not speak to him for a fortnight. Arthur Mitchell understood that severe discipline and gave to others what had been given to him.

He asked the young Len Hutton if he had got six-inch nails in his boots after Len had thought he had fielded well on a particularly gruelling day at The Oval, and when Hutton was later moved into the slips Mitchell did not speak to him for half an hour and then asked, 'What are you doing here? It took me ten years to get here.'

Mitchell played for England against India in 1933–4, but his famous Test match was against South Africa at Headingley in 1935. He was not an original choice and he was gardening when the news came that he was to go to Headingley immediately as he was needed by England. He made 58 and 72, but he was to play only twice more for his country.

The best assessment of his batting came from his team-mate Maurice Leyland. They were in a group talking to an eminent writer on the game, not identified, but almost certainly Cardus, when Arthur Mitchell interrupted. 'Mr X, I don't like tha writing; it's too flowery,' he said. Leyland, annoyed at the intrusion, retorted, 'And that's more than anyone would say of tha batting, Arthur.'

But it is as a fielder that 'Ticker' Mitchell is best

Herbert Sutcliffe, immaculate as always, walks out to bat at Scarborough, 1938

'Ticker' Mitchell takes another catch; he took 438 in his career and 172 of these off the bowling of Hedley Verity

Len Hutton takes a boundary off the bowling of Cave during his innings of 101. England *v* New Zealand at Headingley, Leeds, 1949

remembered. He was an uncompromising character, but, as Ken Kelly insists, he was scrupulously fair and would never dream of claiming a catch unless he was certain the batsman was out. He had prehensile hands and telescopic arms and he was outstanding anywhere in the field, but it was in the silly positions that he excelled most and where he took some memorable catches.

It was said that he would die rather than drop a catch off the bowling of Hedley Verity. There is a story that in his early days Mitchell dived to take a blinding catch and the only praise he got from his Yorkshire team-mates was 'Gerrup, they's making a spectacle o' theeself.' Later the remark was attributed to Mitchell himself and it was claimed that he made it to a fielder who took a spectacular catch off his occasional bowling. Either way it confirms that the man abhorred anything that could be construed as ostentation.

If Arthur Mitchell was a forbidding, unapproachable hero for the young Ken Kelly embarking on a career as a cricket photographer, then Len Hutton, only just his senior, was one with whom he could identify. Kelly

found Hutton shy and retiring. He had come into the game young and found himself 'a young, but great player' among his own boyhood heroes. It was not an easy position for a talented young man among famous players, but Hutton learned much as he sat and listened, and it was these years of listening that helped him to become the astute tactician and brilliant player that he was after the war, in spite of ill-health.

Ken Kelly insists that Hutton was a product of that era that listened to the experienced players and learned from them, even to the extent of imitating the shots that they played. Kelly is also quick to point out that Len Hutton played with a bat that weighed 2lb 2oz or 2lb 3oz and that he relied upon guiding and placing the ball for his runs, not upon bludgeoning with a 3lb bat – which is hard to lift and has taken subtlety and art from batting.

Hutton's career transcended World War II. In 1938 he made a century on his first appearance against Australia and a Test record 364 later in the same series. In the post-war period he captained England when they regained the Ashes and when they held on to them. He continues to serve the game as a most perceptive commentator and it is impossible to restrict him to a time or place, for, like all great men, he suggests a timelessness and an unwillingness to be restricted.

If Hutton achieved a universality, Arthur Wood remained fixedly in Yorkshire. 'He was', says Ken Kelly, 'an earlier version of Godfrey Evans, capable of lifting the side on and off the field with a quip or a funny remark.' He was not only a great team man, but a first-rate wicket-keeper in the days when stumpers spent as much time standing up as back, and, like all great practitioners of the art, he had a rich sense of humour.

It was Wood who was credited with a comment that has since passed into common coinage. When 'Jock' Cameron, the South African, hit Hedley Verity for 30 runs in one over at Sheffield in 1935, Arthur Wood said to the spinner, 'You've got him in two minds, Hedley, he doesn't know whether to hit you for four or six!'

Wood was thirty before he claimed a place in the Yorkshire side and ten years later, when Les Ames was injured, he was picked to play for England against Australia at The Oval. He celebrated by travelling down from Yorkshire to London in a taxi cab. He became the fifth Yorkshireman in the side and when he went in England were 770 for 6. He hit 53 and when he came out he uttered the immortal lines, 'I'm always at my best in a crisis.'

In his last Test match, against the West Indies at The Oval in 1939, the last to be played for seven years, he ended Constantine's volatile innings. The all-rounder swung at the ball and sent it soaring high over Wood's head. The wicket-keeper sprinted back and took the catch at long-leg. 'It's a good job I were standing back,' he gasped.

He was fifty years old when he played his last game

and by that time thirty per cent of his victims had been stumpings.

The majority of his catches had come from the fast-medium pace bowling of Bill Bowes, the spearhead of the Yorkshire attack. Bowes ambled to the wicket in a deceptively easy manner, but he used his great height and his broad shoulders to the full. He was relentlessly accurate and swung the ball late at a lively pace. He could make the ball kick and bounce and on occasions he indulged in leg-theory. He began his career on the MCC ground staff, graduated to his home county and dominated their new ball attack for a decade.

Bowes has the air of an academic, and the air is not deceptive. He used to keep a book in which he noted the strengths and weaknesses of batsmen, field-placings suitable for them and the ways in which he was most likely to get them out. His scholarly attitude is laced with Yorkshire common sense, exemplified by

Bill Bowes (like the cartoon horse 'Tishy') crosses his legs as he goes into the stride

his persuasive comments on the game as a journalist and writer. Like Ken Kelly, he began his career as a journalist on the *Yorkshire Evening News* where he was a great help to other journalists and to photographers.

His values are firm and honest, no nonsense. Recently he was fêted by a television company who wanted him to make comments on a programme that they were producing. He was taken to a pub that serves a good lunch menu and his host asked him what he would like. He peered at the blackboard on which the menu was written and said, 'Duck – ah, duck.' Then he readjusted his glasses and looked again. 'Five pounds. Five pounds for duck. Not bloody likely, I'll have something else.'

Ken Kelly's father used to drink in the Original Oak, the public house opposite St Michael's Church and close to the Headingley ground. He started taking his son there when the lad was about fifteen, and, sitting in the corner, sipping a soft drink in the early days, the boy was able to watch his Yorkshire heroes who frequented the pub. There were so many good players striving to get into the Yorkshire first team in the 1930s that when a regular was injured he would often keep quiet about the injury and play on for fear of losing his place in the side, and the wages that went with it. 'Bright' Heyhurst, the Yorkshire masseur, often treated players in the Original Oak so that neither the captain nor any of the officials were aware that they were injured.

It was in the Original Oak that Ken Kelly saw his greatest hero, Maurice Leyland, with the help of Heyhurst, treat himself for a suspected hairline fracture of a finger. Using a pint of the local brew as anaesthetic, he bound the bad finger against the next finger and then he was ready to play on. He was a small man with a big heart, a player for all pitches and a batsman for all situations. Playing cricket was his life and nothing was going to stop him.

Quick-footed, bright-eyed, good-humoured and unconquerably defiant, Leyland was all that was good in cricket and he relished a fight. He was a left-handed batsman who could hit hard and offer a broad defence. He would stand motionless at the crease as the bowler advanced. His mind, like his body, was still. There was no fretting, no impatience. He breathed defiance and he had a sense of imperturbability which bordered on genius, but there was always an air of fun about him. It was said that he was at his best in foul weather on a bad wicket, which says much for the man who was later a great source of strength and encouragement to young players as the county coach.

He was Ken Kelly's first hero as a boy, and first loves are never really replaced. The last time that the photographer saw Maurice Leyland, or Morris as he was actually christened, was in the bar at Scarborough during the Festival. By then Leyland had Parkinson's disease and it was affecting him badly. 'I could not bear to see my former idol in this way,' says Kelly, 'so I stopped going to the Scarborough Festival and started to go to Hastings instead, preferring to remember Leyland in his prime, a great man and a great player.'

If Leyland and Bradman took the first two places in Kelly's list of heroes then Hedley Verity was very close to them, and he would be placed only behind Leyland in a young man's enthusiasms because he was an introvert rather than the extrovert and busy person that Leyland was. A scholarly bowler and a complete gentleman in manner and demeanour, Hedley Verity followed the great tradition of Yorkshire slow left-arm bowlers, the tradition of Peate, Peel and Rhodes. He bowled at a pace akin to Derek Underwood's and, like the Kent man, he was always naggingly accurate.

In his club cricket Ken Kelly was an accurate off-spin bowler who lost his accuracy if he tried to spin the ball too much. Verity was fulsome in praise and helpful with advice, saying that Kelly's hands and length of

Maurice Leyland at Headingley in 1938

fingers were not appropriate for trying to spin the ball too much and he should concentrate on accuracy. His advice was that accuracy was everything to certain types of spin bowlers and that they should concentrate on length and flight and use the crease to upset the batsmen. He was particularly anxious that a young bowler should develop the 'long ball', the ball bowled from behind the crease, so that the batsman was kept guessing all the time.

He bowled as though all depended upon him and on a wicket that gave him a hint of assistance he was unplayable; but he never felt in need of a helpful wicket, never complained at what he was presented with, and to a young player and a young photographer, he was helpful and charming. He was a man who inspired the love of others.

In 1932, against Nottinghamshire at Headingley, Verity took all 10 wickets for 10 runs, the most outstanding first-class bowling feat ever recorded. J. L. Carr, the prize-winning novelist, then a schoolboy, had left the ground early fearing rain and has now condemned himself to a lifetime of bitter remorse!

It was not to be Verity's last great bowling performance. He averaged 196 wickets a season in his ten-year career and on 1 September 1939, in Jim Parks' Benefit Match at Hove, he took 7 Sussex second innings wickets for 9 runs in six overs as the home side were bowled out for 33. Yorkshire won by 9 wickets and took the Championship. Two days later war broke out and they were not to play another first-class match for six years.

Ken Kelly joined the Royal Navy where there was little time to play cricket or to indulge in photography, no private cameras being allowed to combat personnel in the type of combined special operations in which he was engaged. His early service life was confined to training in telegraphy and coding, and later came a combined operations assault course.

At first seeing service at sea, Kelly spent the last two-thirds of the war in the Mediterranean sector, being engaged in the landings in North Africa, Sicily and Italy, and later in special operations in other areas of the Mediterranean.

Hedley Verity was commissioned in the Green Howards. He was in the Eighth Army's attack on Sicily in 1943. He was hit as he led his company through a cornfield and his last reported words were 'Keep going', an apt motto for his life. He died of his wounds in a prisoner-of-war camp. His close friend Bill Bowes, also a prisoner of war, heard the news of Hedley's death from a Canadian airman who had just been shot down and captured and said that he had heard that Verity 'must have been a great guy'.

When Verity was wounded Ken Kelly was in action near Catania, Sicily, not far from the scene, and he read of his idol's death at a later date in the *Eighth Army News*, the army newspaper. At a time when friends and colleagues were being killed daily it seemed the saddest death of all. 'It was hard to believe that he would never again give me advice, that Yorkshire and England would never have his services again and that the cricketing public would never again see his like.'

An era of Yorkshire greatness had come to an end and with it had ended the first phase of Ken Kelly's apprenticeship as a cricket photographer. Yet already the second stage of his career was being shaped, albeit unbeknown to him. Later in the war he watched a match at Bari in Italy and chatted to two players, 'Tom' Dollery and Tom Pritchard, who were to be mainstays in Warwickshire's Championship side in 1951. Dollery was to captain that side and Pritchard, a New Zealander, and a fine fast bowler, promised Dollery that he would come to England after the war and play for Warwickshire. He kept his promise although it cost him a Test career.

After the war Kelly went back to the *Yorkshire Evening News* as general newspaper photographer at seven pounds a week. There were now more lenses on the market, but there were not the monetary rewards in cricket photography to be able to buy them. The 'Long Tom' was still the equipment even if the housing was a little smaller and so easier to handle.

In 1948, the Birmingham Gazette and Despatch Ltd, who owned five newspapers in Birmingham – a morning paper, a morning sports paper, an evening paper, a Saturday sports paper and a Sunday paper – announced that they were having a 'Long Tom' made and needed someone to work it who had experience in cricket photography. The position also demanded the normal duties of a general press photographer.

Ken Kelly applied and was interviewed by Harold Crabtree, the chief photographer, who asked him about cricket photography, said that he had seen examples of his work and offered him the job within a few minutes. Before accepting, Kelly asked a favour – that he should always have off the week of the Headingley Test match. Crabtree thought that this request was 'a bit of a cheek', but as Kelly had not missed a Leeds Test since 1930 he understood the condition and agreed. So Ken Kelly was able to return to Headingley every year and be with his old colleagues, Jack Hickes and Harry Fletcher. When Jack Hickes wanted a rest or wanted to take some pictures

Hedley Verity and Maurice Leyland in 1939, just before the fateful war

elsewhere on the ground Kelly would take over the 'Long Tom', not for payment, but simply for the love of Leeds and the game. An apprenticeship will come to an end, but old loves and heroes remain with us for ever.

The three ages of Don Bradman

Above The youthful Don Bradman pictured on his first visit to England. This was a souvenir photograph bought by the young Ken Kelly when he first saw Bradman at Headingley in 1930. *Above centre* Don Bradman as captain of Australia in England for the first time, 1938. The kindly smile conceals one of the greatest tactical brains that the game has known. *Right* Ken Kelly pictures Bradman again on his return to England as captain of the 1948 invincible Australian side. *Above far right* Bradman leaves England from Tilbury, never to play Test cricket again

Below Traditionally the Australian tour began at Worcester. The visitors were given the type of welcome usually reserved for royalty. They were met at Shrub Hill station by the Mayor of Worcester, who in 1948 was Councillor J. B. Edwards. The Mayor shakes Bradman's hand to the delight of the Worcestershire skipper, A. F. T. (Alan) White, on the left and the Chief Constable of Worcestershire, Mr E. Tinkler. Keith Miller peeps over White's shoulder and Bradman holds the small leather case which contained his fan mail, all of which he continues to answer personally every day

A happy picture of Don Bradman taken at Bramall Lane, Sheffield, in 1948. A modest and shy man, but a helpful and considerate one, Bradman was walking to the wicket, eyes ahead, concentrating on the job about to be done. On this occasion photographers Harry Fletcher, Jack Hickes and Ken Kelly became entangled as they changed plate holders and wound the shutter whilst walking backwards in an attempt to photograph Bradman. Bradman smiled and slowed his walk in an effort to give the photographers time to recover. It was a kindly gesture, but it did not distract Bradman from the batting task that lay ahead. He scored 54 and 86 on an uncertain wicket and helped Australia to have the better of a drawn game. The picture shown is the one taken by Harry Fletcher

Don Bradman begins his last tour of England with 107 at Worcester in 1948. During this match, Ken Kelly worked alongside George Frankland, whom he regarded as the father of modern cricket photography, for the first time. Frankland was one against whom all other photographers measured themselves so that for Kelly it was a testing time. As only one picture could be taken at a time, shutter releases were often timed so that two or three photographers ended up with almost the same picture. Kelly's work compared favourably with the master's and he was well satisfied with his first encounter with George Frankland

19

Above Bradman walks out at Headingley for the last time (*Photograph by Harry Fletcher, Yorkshire Post*)

Left Jack Hickes' award-winning picture of the record crowd at Headingley, July 1948, titled 'The crowd within and the crowd without'

Arthur Morris on his way to 182

Headingley, 1948

In 1948, Don Bradman led to England what many consider to be the strongest combination of cricketers ever to have visited these shores.

Australia overwhelmed England at Trent Bridge and at Lord's, but the match at Old Trafford was drawn and England had hopes of recovery. These hopes appeared about to be realised at Headingley where the teams met for the fourth Test at the end of July. Yardley, the England captain, declared and asked Australia to score 404 to win on a turning wicket on the last day. Inspired by Bradman, Australia won a historic victory by 7 wickets with fifteen minutes of playing time still remaining.

During the five days, 158,000 people, a record for any match in England, watched the cricket. It was a farewell tribute to the greatest batsman that the world has ever seen.

Jack Hickes, an outstanding photographer and colleague of Ken Kelly's, who chose to spend his professional life with the *Yorkshire Evening News*, noticed the massive crowd which, even though the gates had long been closed, still encircled the ground. Hickes was determined to capture a picture of them. He photographed the crowd in St Michael's Lane imbibing the atmosphere in hope while those inside watched the start of play. The picture, (*left*), one of the most remarkable of cricket photographs, is a memorable tribute to an outstanding photographer.

Don Bradman walks out to bat at Headingley for the last time. He is patted lovingly by one of the many boys to whom he was a hero. He never disappointed his audience.

Bradman responded to the ovation given him by his admirers in Yorkshire with an innings of 173 not out which brought Australia a memorable victory. It was to be Bradman's last Test century; indeed, he made his last runs in Test cricket. In fifty-two Test matches, he scored 6,996 runs and hit twenty-nine centuries.

Bradman shared a second wicket stand of 301 with the elegant left-handed opener Arthur Morris. Morris, powerfully dismissive of anything short on the leg-side, scored 182.

In the first innings, Headingley had glimpsed a new hero who was also a left-hander. Neil Harvey, nineteen years old, was playing his first Test match in England. He was applauded all the way to the pavilion, running the gauntlet of admirers, after he had scored 112.

Above Bradman on the way to his last Test century

Neil Harvey, nineteen years old, scores 112, his first century against England but his second successive Test century

Ken Kelly arrives at Birmingham

If Ken Kelly had been fortunate to be born in Leeds and grow up amid a period of Yorkshire greatness, then he was equally fortunate to move to Birmingham in 1948 at a time when Warwickshire were about to embark on the most illustrious stage of their history. Kelly was employed by the Birmingham Gazette and Despatch Ltd because the group had had a 'Long Tom' made and needed an experienced hand to use it. Not many photographers had used this type of camera, so Kelly was not surprised when he obtained the new appointment.

He left his native Yorkshire with the knowledge that his experience with the *Yorkshire Evening News* would be invaluable. It gave him full confidence in his ability to fulfil his future ambitions.

Whilst he would travel about the country covering cricket, his main day-to-day work would be in the Midlands, mainly Warwickshire, but Worcestershire as well. As it was 'Australian Year', the most important in any cricket calendar, this meant coverage of the first match of the tour, which was traditionally played at Worcester.

New horizons were in the sights of the photographer about to embark on a new phase of his career. For Kelly, it was to be a far more satisfying and rewarding experience than anything he could have ever hoped for.

The Warwickshire captaincy in 1948 was shared by Ron Mauldesley and 'Tom' Dollery, but the following year Dollery became sole captain. He was a professional and the move was a revolutionary one, looked upon with horror in some quarters. In 1948, Warwickshire had finished seventh, in both 1949 and 1950 they were fourth, and in 1951 they took the Championship for the first time since 1911.

Dollery must be given the credit for much of the success. He was instantly warm and welcoming to

Tom Pritchard

'Tom' Dollery

Kelly, inviting him, as the local photographer, to eat and travel with the team whenever he wished. He was an honest and forthright captain who played for the love of the game, and he remains respected by all who have known him. Jack Bannister, who joined Warwickshire as a young professional in 1950, reflected on Dollery more than thirty years later and wrote, 'He taught me more in five years than I learned in another fifteen years in county cricket, and he was head and shoulders above any captain I have seen since. His ability to read a game was peerless.'

Dollery said of the side that he led to the Championship in 1951, 'Eric Hollies apart, we were a team of extraordinary ordinary cricketers.'

Hollies was one of the greatest of leg-spinners, the man who bowled Bradman for a duck in the great man's final Test innings. He took 2,323 wickets in first-class cricket and he was loved in Warwickshire. Indeed, the whole side under Dollery was a happy and popular one. He got the best out of his men, recognising their talents and the vital contributions that each could make. He brought Tom Pritchard to England and assured the committee that Tom would take a hundred wickets in his first full season of county cricket. They were sceptical, but Pritchard's first full season saw him take 172 wickets.

Fred Gardner was the solid rock on which the innings was founded and Alan Townsend could always be relied upon for late runs, and to catch anything and everything that came near him. His third dimension was as a medium-pace bowler of more than average ability.

Grove was the relentless medium-pace opening partner for Pritchard while, for all too brief a period, the slow left-arm of Ray Weeks could turn the course of a game, as, indeed, could Wolton's occasional off-spin.

Eric Hollies

Behind the stumps was Dick Spooner, an effervescent keeper and a left-handed batsman who could give the innings a very brisk start. To balance any impetuosity was the older head of Jimmy Ord, a middle-order batsman of conservative temperament.

A band of 'extraordinary ordinary cricketers' they may have been, but above all they played the game with joy and gave pleasure wherever they went.

The ultimate reward for Warwickshire perhaps was that, mainly through the efforts of secretary Leslie Deakins, in 1957, Test cricket returned to Edgbaston after an interval of twenty-eight years.

Dollery's own career, which had begun in 1933, was hampered by the war. He had played for Berkshire when he was fifteen and for Warwickshire when he was twenty. He was twenty-five when the war broke out and on the threshold of the England side, but eventually he was to play in only four Test matches, a cruel injustice to a man who was for many years the most consistent right-handed batsman in the country with a wide range of shots.

He retired in 1955 and was succeeded as captain by Eric Hollies, who was then forty-three years old. Hollies accepted the captaincy only as a temporary appointment until Mike Smith became available to lead the side in 1957.

Mike Smith had a splendid career at Oxford where he scored centuries in three successive varsity matches. He played rugby for England and played his first county cricket for Leicestershire, but his years with Warwickshire were golden ones. He led Warwickshire for ten years and in the first six of those he scored more than two thousand runs each season. In 1959, he scored 3,245 runs and, in all, he was to pass a thousand runs in a season twenty times, including once overseas. Allied to his consistent and punishing batting was his brilliance as a fielder, mainly at short-leg, and he took 592 catches in his career. He captained England as well as Warwickshire and no captain has been more popular with his men.

The Warwickshire innings was now opened by Fred Gardner and Norman Horner, the aggression of the Yorkshire-born Horner balancing the more careful approach of Gardner. In 1954, 'Billy' Ibadulla had arrived from Pakistan to give stability to the batting and he and Horner shared an unbroken stand of 377 for the first wicket against Surrey at The Oval in 1960. This is still the highest unbroken first wicket stand ever recorded in English first-class cricket and Horner hit the only double century of his career.

Cartwright and Stewart were others to emerge at this time in a side where the bowling was dominated by the whole-hearted Jack Bannister. Barber from Lancashire, David Brown and Dennis Amiss heralded the sixties, but by then cricket in Warwickshire had been firmly re-established and Test status regained, for Edgbaston was quickly becoming the best appointed ground in the country.

The fifties had been a particularly happy time for Ken Kelly, who was welcomed by the side and accepted by them as their extra twelfth man.

M. J. K. Smith

'Tom' Dollery

Horace Edgar Dollery's captaincy of Warwickshire from 1948 to 1955 – he was joint captain in his first year – has become part of Warwickshire and Midland folklore. He scored 24,413 runs in his career which was blighted by the war. He was the first appointed professional captain and he carried out the job with intelligence, humour, dignity and integrity, and he led by example, never asking others to do what he was not prepared to do himself. His philosophy of the game was to enjoy it in such a way that all who watched would enjoy it too. Dollery had been chosen for MCC's tour of India in 1939–40, but the tour was cancelled because of the war, so delaying his Test debut for eight years and he was to play only four times for England with little success. His first-class career continued until 1955 when he was forty-one. He had already taken over the White Horse Inn at Curdworth before he gave up playing.

Dollery hits to leg during his century against Lancashire at Edgbaston in 1951, the Championship year. Ken Grieves is at slip, Alan Wilson is the wicket-keeper

Left Dollery, an occasional wicket-keeper, was an excellent slip fielder. Here he dives to take a one-handed catch to dismiss Alex Thompson of Middlesex in 1953

In his occasional wicket-keeping role, Dollery stumps Desmond Eagar off Hollies in 1951. He took the ball between the left palm and the right glove, and the wicket was broken with the Hampshire skipper down, and out. The ball flew into the air after the wicket was broken, so it was a fair stumping

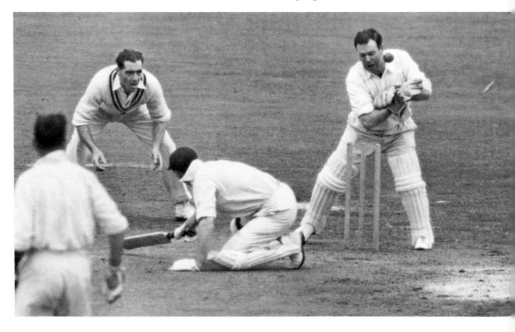

It was obvious that Dollery's first customers at the White Horse Inn had to be Eric Hollies (with glass raised) and Charlie Grove. Dollery is serving his two friends at opening time when he took over the pub in January, 1954. Dollery was a very successful publican and was in the trade until his retirement in 1984. In his years with Warwickshire, particularly as captain, he inspired a great spirit of loyalty and affection in the club, and, above all, a sense of joy in playing cricket. In the Championship year of 1951 there was much exciting cricket

Below Hugo Yarnold of Worcestershire has attempted to play Hollies from the crease and has been caught by Gardner, obscured in the photograph. Ord and Townsend are about to congratulate Gardner. Dollery applauds and Spooner looks heavenwards in delight. Warwickshire won this game with two minutes to spare

Eric Hollies

Eric Hollies was one of the great leg-spinners in cricket history. He will always be remembered as the man who bowled Bradman for a 'duck' in the Don's last Test match; one of Hollies' 2,323 wickets in first-class cricket. Fourteen times the leg-spinner took one hundred or more wickets in a season. He played for Warwickshire from 1932 to 1957 and appeared in thirteen Test matches between 1935 and 1950. In 1946, at Edgbaston, he took all 10 Nottinghamshire wickets for 49 runs; seven of them were bowled and three lbw.

Left Hollies spinning with enthusiasm

A picture of Hollies on his retirement in 1957, with his impressive array of trophies. On his right is his wife 'Ciss', and on his left his daughter Jacqueline. Hollies is wearing an Australian cap which was given to him by Arthur Morris, the Australian opener and vice-captain

An exciting end to the 1954 season at Edgbaston when Warwickshire beat Glamorgan by 56 runs with only a few minutes remaining. Hollies wheels to the umpire in appeal as he traps Haydn Davies lbw for the ninth wicket of the innings. Jim McConnon, the England off-spinner, is the non-striking batsman

Alan Townsend

Alan Townsend played for Warwickshire from 1948 to 1960. He was a reliable right-handed batsman, a medium-pace bowler and an outstanding slip fielder. Skipper Dollery said that he could not remember him dropping a catch in the 1951 Championship season. These four pictures show that the art of slip fielding is balance and correct positioning. They were taken during the Warwickshire *v* Yorkshire match at Edgbaston in 1951.

Left Ted Lester of Yorkshire is taken with ease off the bowling of Eric Hollies

Right Another Yorkshireman falls to the Townsend-Hollies combination. The ball loops off the shoulder of Doug Padgett's bat and Townsend, concentration full even on the easiest of chances, moves to take the catch

Left A third Yorkshire victim of the Hollies-Townsend trap. Eric Leadbeater seems hypnotised by Townsend's hands. They draw the ball like a magnet and another slip catch is taken. Leadbeater later moved to Warwickshire

Right Another catch for Townsend. Roy Booth is taken with nonchalant ease off the bowling of Ray Weeks. Townsend took 413 catches in his career, and only Mike Smith has taken more catches for Warwickshire. The other fielders in these pictures are Fred Gardner and wicket-keeper Dick Spooner

Dick Spooner

An enterprising left-handed batsman and wicket-keeper of the highest order, Spooner was brought to Warwickshire in 1948 on the advice of former Test wicket-keeper and coach 'Tiger' Smith. Spooner was already twenty-nine when he made his debut for Warwickshire, his youth having been lost to the war, but he played for the county for eleven years, and, at a time when Godfrey Evans was the dominant keeper in the world, he was still chosen for England in seven Test matches. Spooner is one of the few players who could have been chosen on merit as either batsman or wicket-keeper. He opened the innings on many occasions and, in 1951, he hit 1,767 runs, topping the county averages with 43.09, and dismissed seventy-three batsmen. He hit twelve centuries in all and scored 13,851 first-class runs. He caught 589 and stumped 178 batsmen.

He is seen here sweeping a ball during his maiden first-class century, 122 *v* Worcestershire, at Edgbaston, 26 May, 1951

Below He seems to have whipped off the bails in time to run out George Emmett of Gloucestershire, for the batsman's bat is not grounded. Emmett was given not out, but the usually neat and dapper batsman has certainly had a fright; a very rare occurrence for a player to whom smartness was important and who always remained unruffled

Dick Spooner catches John Langridge of Sussex off the bowling of Eric Hollies. Langridge was a great slip fielder, as was Alan Townsend who is also in the picture. John Langridge later became a first-class umpire

An outstanding picture of a remarkable stumping. Vic Jackson of Leicestershire, an Australian by birth, is behind the crease, but both his feet are off the ground as Spooner breaks the wicket. Fred Gardner is the slip fielder and the bowler was Eric Hollies. The umpire who gave the decision was Harry Elliott, the former Derbyshire wicket-keeper, and he must have been delighted to witness such skill. It was at Edgbaston in Spooner's memorable year, 1951

Below Another example of Dick Spooner's 1951 form as he dives in front of 'Tom' Dollery to catch Ken Smales of Nottinghamshire one-handed. Spooner was left-handed so that he has taken this with his 'weaker' hand. Alan Townsend is at slip and Ray Weeks is at short-leg. Charlie Grove was the bowler and it was his benefit match

New Zealanders

When 'Tom' Dollery was serving with the Central Mediterranean Forces during World War II he met and was impressed by a young New Zealand fast bowler named Tom Pritchard. Dollery persuaded Pritchard to come to England and qualify to play for Warwickshire. He was qualified to play in the County Championship by the middle of 1947, when he was already turned thirty. A strong, genuinely fast bowler, he took 172 wickets in 1948 and for the next five years, which coincided with a time of great Warwickshire success, he was a power in the land. Fast and straight, he often beat batsmen by pace as he has done in the picture (*left*), taken at Edgbaston in 1949, where Laurie Fishlock of Surrey has had his middle stump knocked back. Eric Bedser looks on apprehensively.

Below left Pritchard was also a powerful hitter, as he is demonstrating here plundering the Lancashire attack to the consternation of slip Ken Grieves and wicket-keeper Alan Wilson.

The Warwickshire-New Zealand connection was cemented by the arrival in 1949 of Ray Hitchcock, a middle order left-handed batsman and a useful leg-break and googly bowler. Hitchcock, pictured below in aggressive mood, worked his passage from New Zealand to seek a cricket career with Warwickshire whom he continued to serve loyally off the field when his playing days ended in 1964.

Like many of his countrymen, Hitchcock was a fine rugby player and he was Nuneaton's scrum-half for some seasons. It was possibly his prowess as a rugby player which accounted for Hitchcock being such a reliable and outstanding catcher, a quality he shared with Tom Pritchard.

The years after World War II witnessed a golden period in New Zealand cricket. The side that toured England in 1949 was certainly one of the best that they have ever produced. Opening batsman, left-hander Bert Sutcliffe (*right*) was a player of immense charm and arguably the best batsman that New Zealand has given to the world. Enterprising, cultured and elegant, he was a fine driver and a clean hooker and puller of the ball. The sun always seemed to shine when he was batting.

He hit 17,283 runs in his career and was featured in many records, one of which remains unchallenged. In 1948–9, he opened the Auckland innings against Canterbury with Don Taylor. They put on 220 in the first innings and 286 in the second, the only instance in cricket history of a double century opening partnership in each innings of the same match.

Don Taylor (*below*) played occasionally for Warwickshire between 1949 and 1953, but he was never as successful in England as in New Zealand for whom he played three Test matches. He was perhaps too eager to play his wide range of shots too soon in an innings, an attractive fault.

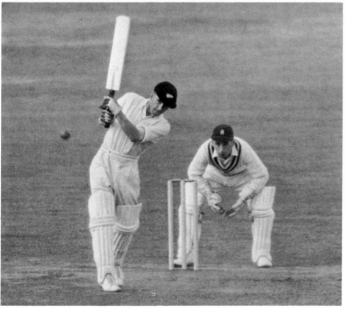

Martin Donnelly was another in the Warwickshire-New Zealand tradition. He played twenty matches for the county between 1948 and 1950 after he had come down from Oxford University. A gifted left-handed batsman who danced to the pitch of the ball and hit with tremendous power for one so short, he played in only seven Test matches, losing years to the war and retiring from cricket to enter business when he was still young. His one Test century was an innings of 206 against England at Lord's when he demoralised the England bowling with a blistering attack. He played cricket for New Zealand, but he was a rugby international for England, playing against Ireland in 1947.

Donnelly, an amiable man, was a ferocious hitter of the ball; at Oxford he hit 142 out of 261 in the Varsity match. As he also hit 162 not out for the Gentlemen against the Players at Lord's, he can be said to share Percy Chapman's record of scoring centuries in the three great fixtures at headquarters.

that it features three of the greatest and most exciting batsmen the world has seen: Clyde Walcott is the wicket-keeper, Everton Weekes is at first slip and Frank Worrell at second slip.

Below Frank Worrell, a master of elegant stroke play, made the West Indians' highest score of the match, 46. The picture reveals the international flavour of the match. 'Tom' Dollery of England watches Worrell play the ball past another Englishman, Fred Gardner. From mid-on Don Taylor of New Zealand watches the path of the ball while in the gully Abdul Hafeez Kardar, once of India, soon to be captain of Pakistan, looks on. The non-striking batsman is Jeff Stollmeyer.

After a tense struggle on a spinner's wicket Warwickshire won by 3 wickets.

Warwickshire *v* West Indies, 1950

In 1950, the West Indies asserted themselves as a powerful Test nation for the first time. Their spin twins, Ramadhin and Valentine, routed England at Lord's, Nottingham and The Oval, and their brilliant batsmen, the three Ws, Worrell, Weekes and Walcott gave joy wherever they went and scored nearly six thousand runs between them. They were beaten only once by a county side and that was when Warwickshire beat them at Edgbaston at the beginning of August.

The Warwickshire hero was Charlie Grove, the medium-pace bowler, who took 8 for 38 in the West Indians' first innings, his best performance in first-class cricket. The tourists were bowled out for 156 and Warwickshire batted to a first innings lead of 128. Charlie Grove, batting in the picture (*above*), contributed 11. The most significant thing about the picture, however, is

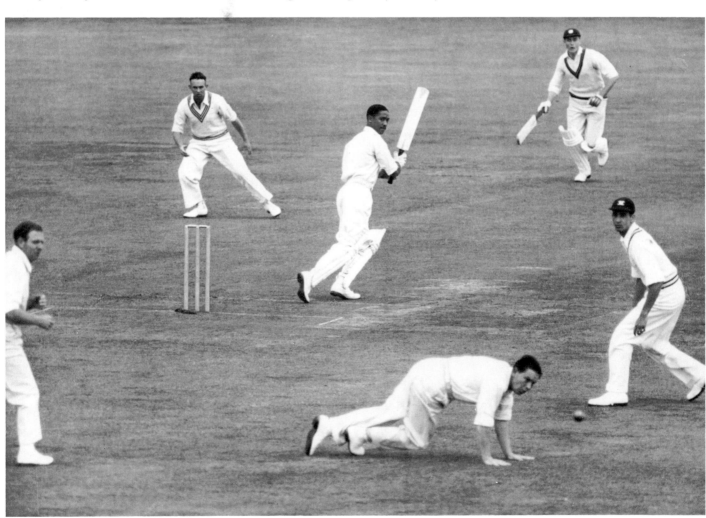

Great South Africans

The 1950s began a memorable period for South African cricket, producing one of the best Test captains that the world has seen, Jack Cheetham. In the picture above, Cheetham has just swept the ball to the boundary during his innings of 116 not out against Warwickshire at Edgbaston, August 1951. Wicket-keeper Esmond Lewis and skipper 'Tom' Dollery watch the ball to the boundary. When Cheetham returned to England four years later it was as captain of the first South African side to level a series against England, in England, after being two matches down in the rubber. Cheetham, an outstanding fielder and one who never allowed his men to lose faith in themselves, inspired South Africa to draw series with a strong Australian side and to beat New Zealand convincingly.

The most exciting batsman in Cheetham's era was Roy McLean. McLean (*right*) was a beautifully balanced player, a cutter and hooker of immense power. If he had a fault, it was his eagerness to score from every ball, but it was a fault that made him very popular with the spectators. In the picture he is hitting Eric Hollies for six and most of his big scores were made at a furious rate. He followed Cheetham's example in the field where he was outstanding on the boundary or close to the wicket, and his enthusiasm for the game epitomised the character of Cheetham's team.

Wicket-keeper John Waite (*below*) came to England in 1951 as reserve to Endean, but he won his way into the side for the first Test and remained South Africa's first-choice keeper for the next fourteen years, becoming the only South African to play in fifty Test matches. He was a good enough batsman to open the innings and score four Test centuries, and his batting, like his keeping, showed immense powers of concentration. In the picture he watches intently as Eric Rowan catches Keith Dollery off the bowling of his brother Athol.

The Golden Boy of Cricket

Denis Compton, the Golden Boy of Cricket, who, for several years after the war, captivated crowds everywhere with the effervescent charm of his cricket. A truly great batsman, he hit eighteen centuries in 1947 and scored 3,816 runs, both records which are unlikely to be beaten. He was hampered, and eventually forced to retire, by a knee injury. A most attractive man, his face was seen all over England at one time as part of a Brylcreem advertisement.

Denis Charles Scott Compton

Career batting: 515 matches, 38,942 runs at
    51.85, 123 centuries
Test batting: 78 matches, 5,807 runs at
    50.06

Below John Warr picks up a bump ball off 'Tom' Dollery as the Compton brothers, big Leslie the wicket-keeper and Denis at slip, look on

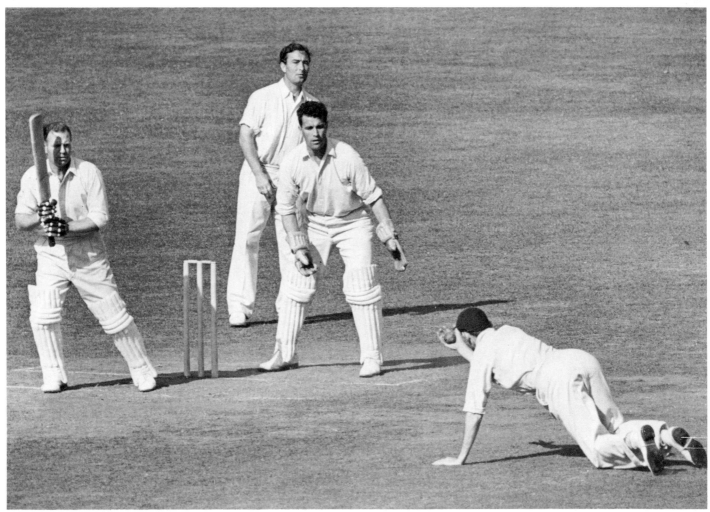

The Great Professional
Len Hutton, the master batsman, goes out to open the Yorkshire innings with Frank Lowson in 1950. A supreme opening batsman, Hutton was groomed by Herbert Sutcliffe and came to take Sutcliffe's place in the England side. One of England's most successful captains, Hutton scored 40,140 runs in first-class cricket with 129 centuries and he hit 6,971 runs in his seventy-nine Test matches. At The Oval, in 1938, he scored a record 364 against Australia. He was knighted in 1956.

Sir Leonard Hutton
Career batting: 513 matches, 40,140 runs at 55.51
Test batting: 79 matches, 6,971 runs at 56.67

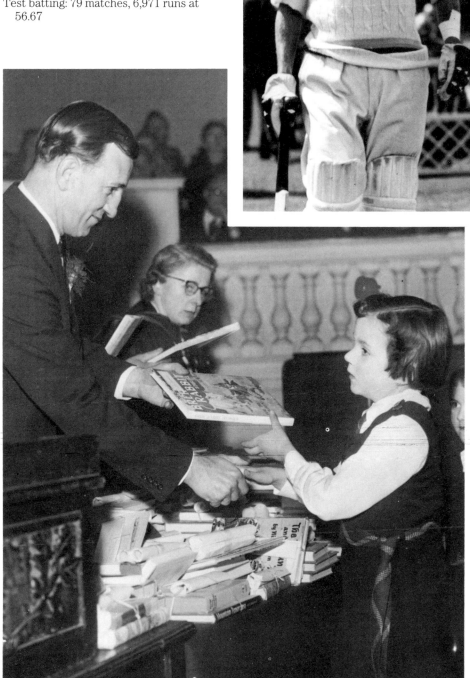

Ever conscious of his social responsibilities, Hutton is seen here distributing the prizes to Greenmore College, Birmingham, March, 1958. Jane Cordwell is the recipient

'Jackie' McGlew

Derrick John McGlew captained South Africa in fourteen of the thirty-four Test matches he played. A dour and tenacious little opening batsman, he made his highest score in Test cricket against New Zealand at Wellington in 1952–3 when he hit 255 not out as South Africa made 524 for 8 declared. New Zealand were then bowled out for 172 in each innings so that McGlew became only the second player in Test history to be on the field for the whole of the match. In 1955, he came to England as vice-captain of the South African side and was the outstanding batsman of the tour, scoring centuries in both the Tests which the South Africans won. In the match against Warwickshire (*left*) he cuts a ball from Hollies past Townsend at slip during his innings of 81. He and Goodard put on 146 for the first wicket. This was less than a fortnight after they had established a South African record for the first wicket with 176 against England at Headingley. In a career that lasted twenty years, he hit 12,170 runs, at an average of 45.92. A brilliant cover field, he took 103 catches.

Vijay Hazare

Vijay Hazare, the most distinguished member of a great cricketing family, plays his famous square cut (*right*) under the appreciative eye of Dick Spooner. Hazare captained India in fourteen Test matches and in the thirty times he played for his country he scored centuries against all the other Test-playing nations that he met on the field. His sixty first-class centuries included two triple centuries, the more remarkable of which was his 309 for The Rest against The Hindus out of a total of 387. His brother played for Mysore and his son and two nephews have played for Baroda. In 1946–7, when playing for Baroda against Holkar, he shared a fourth wicket partnership of 577 with Gul Mahomed, the highest stand for any wicket in the history of first-class cricket. Hazare scored 18,754 runs in first-class cricket at an average of 58.06. He was also a very useful medium-pace bowler as his 595 first-class wickets testify.

Tiger Smith

One of the great men of Warwickshire and England cricket, E. J. 'Tiger' Smith. A wicket-keeper batsman, 'Tiger' (*above*) played for Old England against Warwickshire at Edgbaston in 1951. Smith was sixty-five years old at the time. Jimmy Ord is the batsman

Smith spent most of his life at Edgbaston, and he is seen (*left*) at the opening of the Warwickshire Indoor School in 1956

Below left A letter from P. G. Wodehouse to Roland Ryder shows a picture of Smith and Frank Field (standing) and Percy Jeeves. Jeeves, who was killed in World War I, was a talented all-rounder and author Wodehouse took his name when he created his famous butler

Below Smith, a member of the 1911 Championship side, chats to Dennis Amiss whom he coached and who was a member of the 1972 Championship side. Also pictured is Tom Pritchard, who played in the 1951 Championside side. Smith's playing career lasted from 1904 to 1930, and he scored 16,997 runs and dismissed 878 batsmen

P. G. WODEHOUSE
REMSENBURG
NEW YORK

Oct 26.1967

Dear Mr Ryder.

Yes, you are quite right.

It must have been in 1913 that I paid a visit to my parents in Cheltenham and went to see Warwickshire play Glos on the Cheltenham College ground. I suppose Jeeves's bowling must have impressed me, for I remembered him in 1916, when I was in New York and starting the Jeeves and Bertie saga, and it was just the name I wanted.

I have always thought till lately that he was playing for Gloucestershire that day. (I remember admiring his action very much)

Yours sincerely

P. G. Wodehouse

Roley Jenkins

He played 352 matches for Worcestershire from 1938 to 1958. In the meantime, he scored 10,073 runs and took 1,309 wickets with his leg-breaks and googlies. A hard-hitting batsman, he was renowned most of all for his enthusiastic and tireless bowling. As is shown (*left*), he always bowled with his cap on. He expected to get a wicket every ball, so he schemed to get batsmen out and he took a maiden over as an insult because it meant he was not baiting the batsman. He was one of the last great characters of English cricket, always thinking about the game and always talking about it.

Jenkins was loath to throw his wicket away although he loved to hit the ball and he scored 1,000 runs in a season four times. Twice he did the double, in 1949, when he took 183 wickets, and in 1952. He had much

success for England in South Africa, but in all he played in only nine Tests.

When he felt that he had got his 'mechanics' wrong, as he would say, he would spend as much as six hours bowling in the nets to get them right.

The picture below was taken in 1953 and was one of the British Press Pictures of the Year exhibited by the *Encyclopaedia Britannica*. The photograph shows the Worcestershire skipper, Ronnie Bird, making a spectacular catch to dismiss Ian Thomson of Sussex off Jenkins' bowling. The ball has bounced off the gloves of wicket-keeper Hugo Yarnold and Bird has stopped it with his arms and knocked it up as he falls backwards and completes the catch. George Dews looks on from second slip. Jim Parks is the non-striking batsman and Pothecary is the umpire.

Lindsay Hassett

The 1953 Australians were not perhaps the strongest combination ever to have come to England, but they were beaten only once on the tour, when England regained the Ashes at The Oval. Their skipper, the diminutive Lindsay Hassett, a popular leader and a batsman with a willingness to attack, played one of the finest innings of his career a week before the final Test at The Oval. On a wicket which was giving assistance to spin, Australia were asked to make 165 runs to win in 170 minutes. McDonald, Craig, Hole, Miller and de Courcy all succumbed to the wiles of Hollies and Wolton, eager to snatch a Warwickshire victory for the Edgbaston crowd. Hassett alone defied them. Unwilling to see his side beaten so close to the deciding Test, he curbed his natural aggression and scored 21 not out in the 170 minutes of the innings so that the Australians closed at 53 for 5 and the match was drawn. *Above* Hassett plays a ball from Hollies past Townsend as wicket-keeper Spooner looks on. *Left* Hassett leaves the field with Richie Benaud, applauded by rival skipper 'Tom' Dollery.

39

The Great English Fast Bowlers

The 1950s saw a generation of outstanding English fast bowlers come to the fore and assert superiority over the other Test-playing nations. The three greatest fast bowlers of the period, Trueman, Statham and Tyson, were men of different backgrounds and different characters.

No man was more popular with the public, or indeed with many who played with him, than 'Fiery' Fred Trueman. The picture on the left, published only once before, in the *Birmingham Gazette* the morning after it was taken, is much admired by Trueman himself. It was taken at Coventry in 1954 when Trueman spearheaded Yorkshire to a 10-wicket victory over Warwickshire by taking 7 for 67 in Warwickshire's first innings.

The picture was taken from square to the wicket and shows Trueman using every ounce of energy in his delivery stride. The left arm is flung straight in the air at the moment before release and the eyes are looking over the left shoulder. The weight is being transferred from right foot to left foot in one huge delivery stride. The right arm is cocked in anticipation of moving into the bowling arc to release the ball.

The balance is perfect. The strength is used to its utmost, but, in the precision of technique, economical to the stamina of the bowler. This is the classic action side-on.

In a career that was not without controversy and which lasted for twenty years, Trueman's appetite for the game remained undiminished. He became the first Englishman to take 300 wickets in Test cricket when he had Neil Hawke caught at slip off his lethal late outswingers at The Oval in 1964.

He ended with 307 Test wickets, but he should have taken many more, for he was omitted from tours and sides when lesser men were played. The image of his black hair flowing wildly as he ran briskly and smoothly to the wicket, eagerly seeking another victim, is stamped indelibly on the minds of all those who saw him.

In the majority of Test matches in which he played, Fred Trueman's opening partner with the new ball was Brian Statham (*top right*). Statham was the most accurate and reliable of bowlers, honest in endeavour, but with an ability to frustrate the batsman and move the ball late that marked him above the ordinary, for he was one of the world's best fast bowlers.

Frederick Sewards Trueman
Career bowling: 603 matches, 2,304 wickets at 18.29
Test bowling: 67 matches, 307 wickets at 21.57

John Brian Statham
Career bowling: 559 matches, 2,260 wickets at 16.36
Test bowling: 70 matches, 252 wickets at 24.84

Frank Holmes Tyson
Career bowling: 244 matches, 767 wickets at 20.89
Test bowling: 17 matches, 76 wickets at 18.56

Loose-limbed, he bowled with a smooth action, nagging away relentlessly at the batsman's wicket on an unerring length and moving the ball quickly off the seam. The fluidity of his action can be seen in the photograph where the right hand has followed through to a point where it is almost touching the left calf. The full weight of the body has gone into the delivery.

The umpire in the picture is Bill Copson, the former Derbyshire fast bowler. A strong, attacking bowler, the red-haired Copson played a vital part in Derbyshire's one County Championship title, in 1936, when he took 160 wickets. He played three times for England, but his career was hindered by the war.

It was said in the 1930s that if you needed a fast bowler, all you had to do was shout down a mine shaft and one would come up. This was Copson's beginning for he was a miner until the General Strike in 1926 after which he concentrated on cricket and worked his way up to county level.

Although Trueman was Statham's usual partner in Test cricket, for a brief period it was Frank Tyson (*below*) who opened the England bowling. Like Statham, Tyson is a Lancastrian, but his first-class career, after reading English at Durham University, was spent with Northants. In fact, he played for only eight years, but in that time he gained the reputation of being one of the fastest, if not *the* fastest, bowlers of all time and was nicknamed 'Typhoon'.

The ferocity of his delivery can be seen from the picture. Every muscle is in use, the right foot takes the strain, the right arm is straight ready for delivery and the left leg kicks out menacingly. This photograph was taken in 1954, some months before Tyson went to Australia with Len Hutton's side. He took 1 for 160 in twenty-nine overs in the first Test match at Brisbane, but from there on, he devastated the Australians. His 7 for 27 in the second innings of the third Test at Melbourne is still considered the fastest and most frightening sustained spell of fast bowling seen in Australia.

Like Larwood, his renowned predecessor, Tyson emigrated to Australia where he has been teacher, coach, journalist, writer and commentator.

All-rounders

It was not unusual in the days before the war, and in the period that followed it, for a man to be both a professional cricketer and a professional footballer. Compton, Edrich, Willie Watson and, more recently, Chris Balderstone were among those who excelled at both games. Jack Flavell, the Worcestershire fast bowler who took 1,529 wickets in a career which lasted until 1967, played four times for England as a cricketer and for some time held a regular place as full-back for Walsall. The fiery Flavell is seen bowling (*top right*), and in his Walsall colours (*top left*). He is seen (*middle left*) with England soccer captain Billy Wright, who was offered terms by Worcestershire but who could not take up the engagement because he was chosen to play soccer for England in the winter of 1946, and went on tour with England that summer; he much regretted the fact that the chance of playing county cricket was denied him.

Below Jack Flavell combines both sports, running out Fred Gardner with a right foot drive as Roy Booth looks on excitedly

Warwickshire v Australians, 1956

Left Mike Smith was in the process of qualifying for Warwickshire, ready to take over the captaincy in 1957; he could not play in county matches but was able to play in this tourist match. Here he clips a ball to the leg boundary during his innings of 55. Wicket keeper Len Maddocks follows the flight of the ball

Below In this match the Australians were led by the great all-rounder Keith Miller. He watches impassively as Roly Thompson, a fine support bowler for Jack Bannister, just fails to hold a most difficult chance from Miller off the bowling of rival skipper Eric Hollies

Worcestershire Stalwarts

Reg Perks played for Worcestershire from 1930 to 1955. The first of his 2,233 first-class wickets was that of Jack Hobbs. A fast-medium bowler, he played twice for England in 1939 and although the war ruined his Test career, he served Worcestershire nobly in the post-war period. His career spanned twenty-eight years, and he was appointed Worcestershire's first professional captain.

Perks in action. He bowls to Don Taylor of Warwickshire at Edgbaston, 1951. Bob Wyatt is at slip, Hugo Yarnold is the wicket-keeper and Fred Gardner the non-striking batsman

Right Don Kenyon takes the field. Kenyon first played for Worcestershire in 1946, was appointed captain in 1959 and led the side until his retirement in 1967. He played eight times for England, hit 37,002 runs in first-class cricket and made seventy-four centuries. A man of good sense and natural dignity, he led Worcestershire to their first county championship, and by the time he retired he had scored more runs and hit more centuries than any other player in the county's history

Left Martin Horton, who opened the innings for Worcestershire and was the last opener to do the 'double'. He scored 19,945 runs in his career and took 825 wickets with his off-spin. He played for Worcestershire from 1952 to 1966, and then played first-class cricket in New Zealand for four years before becoming their national coach

Unusual Pictures

The ball becomes lost up Cliff Galdwin's sweater during an innings against Warwickshire at Edgbaston in 1956. He has swung and missed and the shape of the ball is clearly discerned under his sweater. Wicket-keeper Spooner looks bemused, but slip, Clive Leach, has spotted the whereabouts of the ball. Gladwin took his batting seriously, even if others did not. In 1949 he was only 86 runs short of performing the 'double', and in the famous Test against South Africa at Durban in 1948–9, Gladwin ran a leg-bye off the final ball of the game to bring England victory.

Eric Rowan, the South African batsman, has edged a ball from Keith Dollery to 'Tom' Dollery at slip. The fielder has missed the catch with his hands, but has taken the ball between arm and body. As Dollery fell he clasped the ball with his right hand to make it safe and complete the catch. Warwickshire v South Africa at Edgbaston, 1951

Above Keith Andrew, a technically perfect wicket-keeper who played only twice for England because of his limitations as a batsman. *Left* Godfrey Evans, who played in ninety-one Tests for England and made 1,066 dismissals in first-class cricket

Below Jimmy Binks of Yorkshire takes one of the 895 catches he made in first-class cricket. He also made 176 stumpings, but it was as a catcher that he was renowned. His two Test caps were scant reward for consistent brilliance behind the stumps

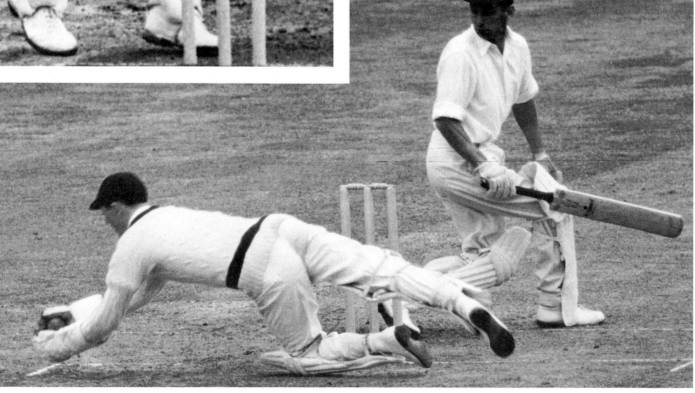

Great Wicket-keepers

In the post-war years Godfrey Evans monopolised the wicket-keeping spot for England until his retirement in 1959. Eight years later he came out of retirement to keep for Kent when Knott was on Test duty. Immediately after the war Paul Gibb of Yorkshire, a Cambridge blue, was seen as number one. Don Brennan played twice for England and was active in Yorkshire committee activities until his recent death. Brennan was of the immaculate school, unfussy in all that he did.

This was certainly a description that also fitted Keith Andrew, considered by many to be the most accomplished wicket-keeper since the war. Now a national coach, Andrew spent his career in the shadow of Evans, Murray, Parks and Binks, all greater run-getters.

The last of the wicket-keepers pictured here is Esmond Lewis. Unable to give as much time to the game as he would have wished, he played for the Gentlemen against the Players and dismissed 119 batsmen in forty-seven first-class matches between 1949 and 1958. He died in 1983.

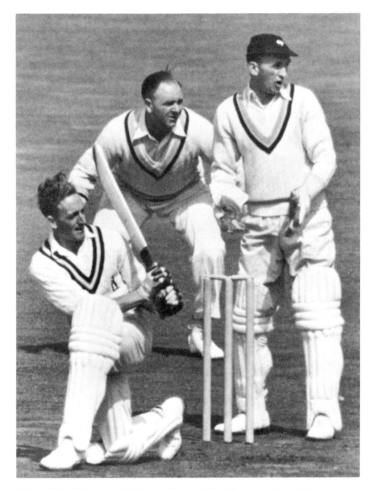

Above Don Brennan is the anxious wicket-keeper in a picture which shows three Yorkshiremen. Norman Horner sweeps Wardle to the boundary and Harry Halliday is the slip. Brennan kept as an amateur for Yorkshire from 1947 to 1953 and had 440 victims in first-class cricket. His two Tests were against South Africa in 1951 as deputy for Godfrey Evans

Above Paul Gibb is the batsman in action for Essex whom he joined as a professional in 1951, after an amateur career with Yorkshire and Cambridge

Right Esmond Lewis stumps Jack Robertson of Middlesex off the medium-pace bowling of Jack Bannister. He was an excitingly agile keeper who caught 8 and stumped 1 on his first-class debut for Warwickshire against Oxford University in 1949

Mike Smith congratulates Jack Bannister as he leaves the field after taking all 10 wickets for 41 runs for Warwickshire against the Combined Services at the Mitchell and Butler's Ground, May, 1959

Jim Stewart, the Warwickshire batsman, is married in Coventry. Fred Trueman, kissing the bride, and Tony Lock, are in attendance

Wilf Wooller has just completed the double and champagne is brought onto the field to celebrate the event. Wooller, a tenacious cricketer, scored 13,593 runs and took 958 wickets in a career which lasted from 1935 to 1962. He captained Glamorgan from 1947 to 1960, and in 1954 he achieved the double of 1,000 runs and 100 wickets

Caught and Dropped

Above Jackie van Geloven of Leicestershire dives to his left at first slip to hold the ball between thumb and second finger to catch Norman Horner at Edgbaston, July, 1959. The Leicestershire wicket-keeper is Ray Julian. He moved as if to attempt the catch, but withheld his right arm so as not to impede van Geloven. The fortunate bowler was Brian Boshier

A missed chance by two of the finest slip fielders the game has seen. Ray Weeks has edged a ball from Brian Statham between Ken Grieves and Geoff Edrich. Grieves has dived to his left, but he realises the catch belongs to Edrich and closes his hand. Edrich, momentarily impeded, misses the chance. Tattersall is at mid-on. Ord is the non-striking batsman. This photograph, taken in 1951, was selected as one of the *Encyclopaedia Britannica*'s British Press Pictures of the Year. It is a rare picture in that Grieves and Edrich took 941 catches between them in first-class cricket and averaged well over one a game

England v West Indies, Edgbaston, 1957

The return of Test cricket to Edgbaston after an absence of twenty-eight years produced one of the most remarkable matches in Test history. It seemed that the supremacy of Ramadhin and Valentine would continue when the home side were bowled out inside four hours for 186. Ramadhin took 7 for 49 and history began to repeat itself as the West Indies built up a big score.

England contained them well for a time and with the West Indies 197 for 5, Walcott making a fine 90 in spite of having to bat with a runner and Sobers scoring 53, the game was quite well balanced, but Frank Worrell then joined 'Collie' Smith in a stand of 190 and the West Indies took total command of the match. England batted again, 288 runs in arrears.

No England batsman had yet been able to 'read' Ramadhin but May and Cowdrey decided to play forward to him, play everything as if it were an off-break and hope that if it was the leg-break, they would miss it.

They put on 411 for the fourth wicket, the highest stand ever made for England. Cowdrey hit 154, and Peter May finished on 285 not out, his highest score in first-class cricket and the highest score ever made by an England captain. Ramadhin bowled ninety-eight overs and took 2 for 179. In their second innings the West Indies made a demoralised 72 for 7 and the match was drawn. The spin menace had been defeated and England won three of the remaining Tests by an innings inside three days.

Left Trevor Bailey becomes Ramadhin's fifth victim in the first innings when he is bowled for 1

Below Peter Richardson, top scorer with 47 in England's first innings, turns a ball past Walcott at backward short-leg. Rohan Kanhai is the wicket-keeper. It was not a sensible job to give the great batsman and Alexander took over later in the series

Opposite above 'Collie' Smith chops late at a ball to the annoyance of Godfrey Evans who has sensed a stumping chance. Smith's 161 was made on his debut against England. A fine batsman whose final flowering was never seen, Smith was tragically killed in a car crash two years later. *Opposite below* Peter May clips the ball away during his historic innings. Rohan Kanhai, later to become a Warwickshire player, is the wicket-keeper

Cricketers who made History in the 1950s
England's leading bowler in the years immediately after World War II, Alec Bedser is one of the greatest medium-pace bowlers of all time. His life has been dedicated to cricket and he has spent more than a quarter of a century as a Test selector, most of that time as chairman. He took 1,924 wickets in his career, 236 of them when playing his fifty-one Test matches. He was one of the very few bowlers ever to have had consistent success against Bradman. He was awarded the OBE for his services to cricket.

Arthur Milton, a player of grace and charm, was the last of the double internationals. He played cricket for Gloucestershire, and played in six matches for England in 1958–9. He also played soccer for Arsenal and Bristol City, and was capped for England in 1951 and 1952. This picture was taken at Edgbaston in 1959, Warwickshire *v* Gloucestershire

Dick and Peter Richardson of Worcester-shire talk to Birmingham Hospitals about the fact that they were both in the England side at Trent Bridge in 1957 and on opposing sides in the Gentlemen *v* Players match at Lord's the same year. Peter Richardson played thirty-four times for England and hit five Test hundreds. He moved to Kent after the 1958 season. Dick Richardson played in only the one Test for England

Somerset Heroes

Harold Gimblett hits a boundary off Perks during his innings of 169 for Somerset at Worcester in May, 1952. Jack Flavell is the fielder. Gimblett was the idol of Somerset until his retirement in 1954, by which time he had hit 23,007 runs with fifty centuries.

Maurice Tremlett is caught Gardner, bowled Townsend at Edgbaston in 1951. Tremlett came into prominence as a quick bowler in 1947 and was in the England side that toured the West Indies the following winter. His bowling did not develop, but his batting did, and he became an attacking middle-order batsman who hit 16,038 runs in his career to complement his worthy 351 wickets. He was an immensely popular man and led Somerset from 1956 to 1959. His son Tim has become an equally successful cricketer with Hampshire

England Stalwarts of the Post-war Era

Tom Graveney (*left*) first played for Gloucestershire in 1948 and he was to play for them throughout the 1950s. The next decade he was to spend with Worcestershire. One of the most consistent and elegant batsmen England has seen, he was unable for some seasons to command a regular place in the Test side because of the high quality of batsmanship at the time. Nevertheless, he played seventy-nine times for England, scoring 4,882 runs, average 44.38, and hitting eleven centuries. In his distinguished first-class career, he hit 122 hundreds and scored 47,793 runs.

Bill Edrich (*below*), like Graveney, did not always please those in authority, and but for this fact and the war, in which he won the DFC, he would have played more than thirty-nine Tests for which he was chosen. A tremendous fighter and a most courageous cricketer, he shared with Denis Compton the golden summer of 1947 when he hit 3,539 runs. He was joint captain of Middlesex in 1951 and 1952 and then sole captain until 1957. He was also a useful medium-pace bowler and an outstanding slip fielder, taking 529 catches in his 571 first-class matches.

Cyril Washbrook (*below left*) was Len Hutton's opening partner immediately after the war and he went on to become the first professional captain of Lancashire, 1954–9. As with Edrich, his career was scarred by the war and he played in only thirty-seven Tests. It seemed that his international career was over in 1950, but six years later, when he himself was a Test selector, his fellow selectors persuaded him to return to the England side against Australia and he scored 98. He scored 34,101 runs in his career and was among the most popular men ever to play for Lancashire, whom he still serves as a committee member.
Below Bill Edrich. A great fighter and entertainer, he was a magnificent slip fielder

Above Tom Graveney. His off-driving was reminiscent of the great Wally Hammond to whom he was the natural successor in the Gloucestershire side. *Below* Cyril Washbrook. Wise and tenacious, he scored 2,569 Test runs, average 42.81, and formed a famous partnership with Len Hutton

To complement batsmen of great talent there were some of the most accomplished bowlers of all time, including the outstanding off-spinner Jim Laker (*above*). He was one of the principle reasons why Surrey dominated the County Championship in the 1950s, and in 1956 he took a record 46 wickets in the Test series against the Australians. His 19 for 90 in the Old Trafford is unlikely ever to be surpassed, and he had already taken all ten Australian wickets when Surrey played the tourists earlier in the year. His main spin partner was Tony Lock, but many considered Johnny Wardle (*top right*) the best left-arm spinner in the country. Wardle left Yorkshire in 1958 after writing some controversial newspaper articles. He had taken 1,846 wickets in his career. Dick Howorth (*below*) was a slow left-arm bowler and a batsman good enough to score 11,479 runs, but the war ruined his career and this fine

player appeared in only five Tests, all in the West Indies. He gave wonderful service to Worcestershire. Bob Barber (*bottom right*) was a fine batsman with Lancashire, Warwickshire and England and perhaps his great potential as a leg-spinner was never fully developed.

Tom Cartwright

Tom Cartwright played first-class cricket for twenty-five years. He began as a batsman, had a successful middle period as an all-rounder and ended almost exclusively as a medium-pace bowler of superb accuracy and telling striking rate.

He first played for Warwickshire, as a batsman only, in 1952, but appeared infrequently over the next few seasons, batting anywhere in the order. Then in 1959 Cartwright took 80 wickets and moved into the top category of medium-pacers. He did the 'double' in 1962 when he made his highest score, 210 against Middlesex at Nuneaton. In all, he scored 13,710 runs and took 1,536 wickets in first-class cricket.

He moved to Somerset in 1970 and played for them until 1976 when he moved to Glamorgan. A year later he became coach to Glamorgan for whom he appeared seven times.

Right Cartwright the bowler

Below Townsend, one of the finest of close-to-the-wicket fieldsmen, dives to catch Slade off Cartwright's bowling. Spooner is the wicket-keeper and Jack Crapp is the umpire

Above Tom Cartwright the batsman in action against Cambridge University. He hit seven centuries in his career

Richardson and Smith
Right Peter Richardson and Mike Smith walk out to open the England innings against New Zealand at Edgbaston in 1958. This was the bespectacled Smith's Test debut and he was out for 0, but he went on to give England yeoman service

'Billy' Ibadulla
Khalid 'Billy' Ibadulla, the Pakistani all-rounder who gave Warwickshire fine service and later became a first-class umpire. He was a dependable opening batsman, scoring 17,039 runs in his career and sharing a first wicket record stand of 377, unbeaten, with Norman Horner against Surrey at The Oval in 1960. Eight years later he shared a record fourth wicket stand of 402 with Rohan Kanhai against Nottinghamshire at Trent Bridge. He bowled both seam and off-breaks (*right*), and took 462 wickets in his career. He played in four Test matches. His son has played for Otago in the Shell Shield in New Zealand.

Ted Dexter

There has been no more regal batsman since World War II than Ted Dexter. In many ways 'Lord' Ted was out of his age, for, a man of multiple talents, he would have fitted easily into the golden age of the Edwardians.

He first played for England while still at Cambridge University and, in all, he played sixty-two Test matches, captaining England against all the major Test-playing countries. He was a batsman of grandeur, handsome and brilliantly aggressive, yet the most memorable of his nine Test centuries were made when he batted to save his side.

In June 1961, England met Australia at Edgbaston for the first time since 1909. The bowling of Mackay and Benaud shot England out for 195 in their first innings and Australia, inspired by a Neil Harvey century, took a lead of 321 by the Saturday evening when they declared, leaving England fifty minutes and two days to bat in miserable conditions in an attempt to save the game

Rain and bad light restricted play on the Saturday evening and on the Monday when Ted Dexter came to the wicket with the score at 93 for 1. On the last day, the sun shone and the Australian bowlers looked forward to exploiting a drying wicket. They were to be disappointed. In one of the most memorable displays of driving seen on the Edgbaston ground, Dexter flayed the Australian attack for five and three quarter hours.

It was a glorious exhibition of the art of batting. He hit thirty-one fours and reached 180 before being stumped by Grout off Simpson eight minutes before the close of play. At the time, it was the highest innings made by an Englishman against Australia since the war.

There was dignity and disdain in Dexter's batting. He struck the ball with the contempt, power and clarity of the aristocrat. In the picture, Grout and Davidson look on in admiration as the bat sweeps through straight and clean to drive Simpson to the boundary in the arc between bowler and mid-off. This was batting in the classical manner.

Edward Ralph Dexter

Dexter was captain of Sussex from 1960 to 1965, and captain of England in thirty Tests, from 1961–2 in India to the series against Australia in 1964. He was also a noted golfer.

Career matches: 327 matches, 21,150 runs at 40.75, highest score 205 with 51 centuries, 419 wickets at 29.92 runs each, 234 catches
Test matches: 4,502 runs at 47.89, 66 wickets at 34.93 each

The Loveliest Ground in England

One of the most beautiful grounds in the world, New Road, Worcester presents a setting most appropriate for English county cricket. This picture, taken in 1955, shows the new scoreboard (opened in 1954) which is now a feature of the ground. The cricket match, with its backcloth of clouds and the cathedral, looking on with dignity, create a tranquil scene.

The ground is most adaptable too, for the River Severn, which skirts it, invariably floods in winter providing opportunities for sailing. In the early 1950s the boys from Kings School, Worcester, forsook their usual sailing place at Tewkesbury to use the facilities that the County Ground had surprisingly given them.

At times the floodwater has frozen, and skating has taken over. It has in fact been a multi-sports stadium, with bowls, tennis, cycling and athletics being staged there. The ground has also been used for outdoor carnivals and displays, as well as open-air religious meetings.

Amiss and Brown

Dennis Amiss and David Brown made their first-class debuts in 1960 and 1961 respectively. The picture of Amiss (*above*) was taken in 1958 when he was recognised as a young batsman with a bright future. David Brown (*below*) now manager of Warwickshire, is shown here on his first-class debut at Edgbaston playing against Derbyshire. He later had great success as a fast-medium bowler for England and captained Warwickshire for three seasons.

M. J. K. Smith

A respected captain of Warwickshire and England at cricket and a fly half who represented England at Rugby Union against Wales, Mike Smith is shown above in Ken Kelly's famous montage picture of the bespectacled sportsman in both his guises. Smith had been a double blue at Oxford and his double international career had been predicted. Ken Kelly anticipated his selection with this picture.

The 1960s and Change

The closure of the *News Chronicle* and of the *Birmingham Gazette* in the early 1960s brought about changes in the lives of many who had been associated with those newspapers, and Ken Kelly was one of those affected. He had worked with two large Fleet Street agencies and had many friends on the two defunct newspapers.

For some time he had believed that he was in need of a change both in his private life and in his work. The upheavals in Fleet Street made that change even more desirable and he decided to travel to Australia and the Pacific, areas which he had long wanted to visit.

The move was to provide the incentive and the development in his work which he had sought. Leaving England in 1962, he spent the next four years working all over the world and widening the range of his art. He did shipboard photography for the P & O lines and took on assignments in the publicity and commercial areas of his work. He contributed pictures to newspapers and magazines and his varied commissions took him far and wide.

He worked with Ed Murrow in New York and Washington and travelled with the King of Malaysia, who was returning from a pilgrimage to Mecca, from Egypt to Penang. He met Sir Robert Menzies, who was convalescing on the SS *Canberra*, and as well as photographing that great politician he shared a friendship with him, spending many hours talking about their common love, cricket.

Whenever it was possible, Ken Kelly watched cricket. He saw matches in the West Indies, Australia and New Zealand, but the photographing of these games was a near-impossibility, for the only equipment available was the 'Long Tom' which was large and heavy and not easy to transport.

It was this fact that made Kelly consider the advances that had been made in photographic equipment in Japan, and a trip there became a necessity. He made several visits and was impressed by the new 400mm lenses that were being produced. These, together with the 2X tele-converters that were also appearing on the market, provided the alternative to the immobility of the 'Long Tom'. In Japan, Ken Kelly purchased a 35mm camera, a 400mm lens and a 2X tele-converter and he first used them in Australia in 1965–6.

With 35mm film not being as fast in emulsion speed as in later years and with dark-room skills not as refined as they were to become later, the initial results

Sydney, January 1966. The first picture taken with 400mm lens, plus 2X tele-converter, purchased in Japan. David Sincock caught by Mike Smith off David Allen. Bob Barber and John Murray look on

were not as good as those of the old 'Long Tom', but the mobility was a compensation for the drop in standard and the pictures were still good enough for newspaper reproduction, so Kelly persevered.

He took his new equipment to the England-Australia Test match in Sydney in January 1966 and set it up close to the local photographer. He shot a roll of film and one of the photographs is reproduced here. It shows Mike Smith, the England skipper, leaping to catch David Sincock off the bowling of David Allen, the Gloucestershire off-spinner. Sincock was one of Allen's four second innings victims as Australia were bowled out for 174 and England won by an innings and 93 runs.

The picture was taken fractionally later than the one taken by the local Sydney photographer. Kelly had not become completely sensitive to the shutter release of the 35mm camera, and the result, technically, in print and picture quality, was not as good as that achieved by the Sydney photographer with his 'Long Tom'. It was good enough, however, to convince Ken Kelly that the teething problems would soon be overcome.

He returned to England and at Edgbaston in 1968 he photographed the whole of the England-Australia Test for the *Birmingham Post* using the 35mm camera. He never returned to his 'Long Tom' and, for Ken Kelly, a new era of cricket photography had started.

Cowdrey's Hundredth Test Match

The England-Australia Test match at Edgbaston in 1968 was significant both to cricket and to Ken Kelly as a photographer. Having experimented with the 35mm camera in Australia, Kelly decided to use it at this Test with a 400mm lens with a 2X Tele-converter that would make it into an 800mm lens. In fact, this meant the end of the use of the 'Long Tom'.

The Test match was Colin Cowdrey's hundredth, and he celebrated the occasion by scoring 104. He was England's captain in this match, but he injured a leg and Tom Graveney took over in the field. Graveney also led England in the next Test at Headingley. Cowdrey pulled a muscle while batting and used Boycott as a runner in the later stages of his innings. He was the first man to play one hundred Test matches and his century was his twenty-first for England. He was to play in fourteen more Tests and score one more century.

Cowdrey plays a ball to leg during his innings of 104. Taber is the wicket-keeper, and Ian Chappell at slip

Cowdrey has taken off his cap to acknowledge the applause of the crowd and the congratulations of the players. Graveney, with whom he shared a stand of 93, claps his bat in appreciation of his colleague

The four pictures on these pages showing Cowdrey acknowledging the applause of the crowd and of the players, were taken within the space of a couple of minutes. No motor-wind was used, but by using the lever-wind which advanced the film and cocked the shutter at the same time, Kelly found that he could easily take this number of pictures. He was next to Dennis Oulds of Central Press who was using a 'Long Tom'. Oulds was one of the finest sports photographers, but he could only take one picture, while Kelly took four. The equipment did not make Kelly a better photographer than Oulds but it widened possibilities and gave him more options.

The two pictures above show Cowdrey touching his cap as he receives the congratulations of Tom Graveney, and Eric Freeman walking to shake hands with Cowdrey. A young Ian Chappell is in the background

Cowdrey walks down the wicket and lifts his bat aloft. Freeman chats to Bill Lawry and Ian Chappell and Bob Cowper applaud

The end of Cowdrey's innings, bowled by Freeman for 104. Perhaps Freeman and Lawry had been discussing a plan to dismiss Cowdrey

England *v* **Australia, Edgbaston, 1968**
These pictures were taken with a 400mm lens, with a 2x tele-
converter which made it into an 800mm lens.

Eric Freeman swings at a Ray Illingworth off-break and is bowled.
Knott lifts his hands in defence or supplication, and Ken
Barrington is poised at slip

Ian Chappell's leg stump is knocked back by a ball from medium-
pace bowler Barry Knight. Knott is ready to take the ball, Graveney
is at slip. Chappell scored 71, Freeman 6. It was Colin Cowdrey's
hundredth Test match and it ended in a draw

Mike Smith in 1959, the season in which he scored 3,245 runs. One of the earlier colour cricket pictures

E. J. 'Tiger' Smith seated in front in the Sydney Barnes Memorial Gate at Edgbaston. Smith kept wicket to the great bowler

Above left Lance Gibbs bowling for Warwickshire vs Northamptonshire in 1971. David Steele is the non-striking batsman

Above Rohan Kanhai batting for Warwickshire vs Worcestershire, 1971. Alan Ormrod at slip, Gordon Wilcock the wicket-keeper

Below right Dennis Amiss in action in 1969

Below John Jamieson in 1969

Alan Ward

Making his first-class debut in 1966 at the age of nineteen, Alan Ward was regarded as the brightest fast bowling prospect England had seen for many years and, in 1969, seemed on the threshold of an outstanding career. Ken Kelly's picture shows the fast bowler in full flow and was judged one of the fifteen best sports photographs of 1970 in the British *Encyclopaedia Britannica* Press Picture of the Year Competition. Very tall and slim, Ward never fulfilled the promise that he had shown. He was carefully nursed by Derbyshire, but he was plagued by injuries and played in only five Test matches between 1969 and 1976. His greatest disappointment was being forced to return home early from Australia in 1970–1 through injury and so missing the glory shared by John Snow and the other England fast bowlers. He played for Leicestershire in 1977 and 1978, but he was unable to command a regular place in the side and, still troubled by injuries, he faded from the game. Ward left a memory of a bowler who, on occasions, could be very fast indeed, but there was an abiding regret at what might have been.

Jim Stewart

He played for Warwickshire from 1955 to 1969, and won a reputation for being an exciting batsman and a great hitter; his first innings of 155 against Lancashire at Blackpool in 1955 included 10 sixes. He hit 7 sixes in his second innings of 125, giving him a total of 17 sixes in one match. He was popular with the crowd for he had an aggressive approach to the game as can be seen from the picture (*left*).

His career with Warwickshire had a sad end. In 1969, either, as Ken Kelly says, by his own wish or at the request of the club, he altered his style completely and became a push-and-run player. It was a change that was ill-received by the spectators, and the happy relationship that Stewart once had with them broke. The push-and-run style was ill-suited to the man and, in becoming a stonewaller, his character seemed to change. He was barracked by the crowd and responded in a way which was uncharacteristic of the younger Stewart and which brought the game into disrepute, which saddened Kelly and many of Stewart's admirers, he was a good all-round sportsman. He also played rugby union football as a centre and full-back for Coventry and Warwickshire.

Below left The stonewaller Stewart pushes forward and Ken Palmer looks on. *Below centre* He stands sullen at the barracking of the crowd. *Below right* Stewart gestures to the crowd in front of the Press Box, a tragic end to the career of a gifted cricketer who gave so much pleasure in his earlier years

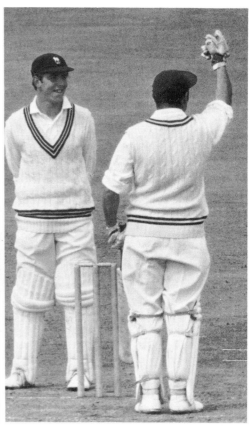

Entertainers

Rohan Kanhai, one of the most exciting batsmen to appear in international cricket. He is shown here batting against India. Farokh Engineer is the wicket-keeper

Rohan Babulal Kanhai
Career batting: 416 matches, 28,774 runs at 49.01
Test batting: 79 matches, 6,227 runs at 47.53
Brian William Luckhurst
Career batting: 388 matches, 22,293 runs at 38.17
Test batting: 21 matches, 1,298 runs at 36.05
John Alexander Jameson
Career batting: 361 matches, 18,941 runs at 33.34
Test batting: 4 matches, 214 runs at 26.75
He was born in Bombay, India, and, had he not been given a cap for England, was thinking of offering his services to India

John Jameson, one of the great crowd pleasers, attacked the bowling from the start of the match and was one of the most exciting opening batsmen of the sixties and seventies

Below Brian Luckhurst, now manager of Kent, a reliable England opener who was never afraid to hit the ball

The D'Oliveira Affair

Basil D'Oliveira reached a high standard as an all-rounder in club cricket in South Africa but, as a Cape Coloured, he found his way to first-class cricket barred in his own country. Encouraged by John Arlott, he came to England where he prospered in Central Lancashire League cricket with Middleton. Five years later, in 1964, he was qualified to play for Worcestershire and such was his advance that he won a place in the England side the following summer. He played in the first Test match against Australia in 1968, but he did not play again until the fifth Test when he came in as replacement for Prideaux. He scored 158, but when the party to tour South Africa that winter was announced his name was not among them. Public and political outcry was great and when Cartwright was forced to withdraw through injury D'Oliveira was invited to tour. Within weeks, Mr Vorster, the South African prime minister, stated that the MCC team was unacceptable as it had been chosen by the 'anti-apartheid' movement. To D'Oliveira, so keen to return to the country whose laws had hindered his progress, it was a grievous blow as it was to the whole of cricket and it heralded the end of South Africa's participation in Test cricket. In South Africa, the leading players demonstrated their eagerness to play against men of all races and colours by leaving the field and issuing a statement during a representative match.

In the midst of all the controversy, D'Oliveira appeared outwardly calm, and he handled the situation with great dignity. In private, his mind must have been in a turmoil, for he is such a deeply caring man. His thoughts must have been for himself, his family and also for the other players chosen for the tour, but who were denied the right to go just as he had been.

It must have taken him some time to overcome the events of 1968, and the cancellation of the South African tour of England in 1970 must have brought back many unhappy memories. On this occasion, a series of England against the Rest of the World was arranged. Five international matches were played; they were termed Test matches at that time, but later the terminology was changed. D'Oliveira found himself playing with and against many of the great names of cricket: from the West Indies came Gary Sobers, Rohan Kanhai, Deryck Murray, Lance Gibbs and Clive Lloyd.

Other overseas players were Mushtaq Mohammad and Intikhab Alam from Pakistan, Farokh Engineer of India, and Graham McKenzie of Australia. Finally, five of the original South African touring team made up the squad: Eddie Barlow, Mike Procter, Barry Richards and the brothers Peter and Graeme Pollock, with one South African born player, Tony Greig, playing for England.

As all the top English players also took part, it was cricket of a very high standard, and the Rest of the World won the series by four matches to one.

Opposite Cricketers of three races play in perfect harmony. Basil D'Oliveira drives. Deryck Murray of the West Indies is wicket-keeper while first slip is white South African Eddie Barlow. This match was played at Edgbaston, and Basil D'Oliveira had scored 110 and 81

Below Mike Procter of South Africa and Gloucestershire, voted Players' Player of the Year in 1969, receives the Hayter Trophy from Gary Sobers at Edgbaston. They are friends and enjoy the ceremony. In the background, John Arlott, D'Oliveira's early helper, watches the proceedings with pleasure

Eddie Barlow (*left*) was one of cricket's great fighters. A tenacious batsman and a right-arm medium-pace bowler, he captained Derbyshire for three seasons and revitalised the county, but he was a fine all-round cricketer for South Africa in thirty Test matches, taking 40 wickets and scoring 2,516 runs. This does not include his performances for Rest of the World XIs, for against England at Headingley, in 1970, he took 4 wickets in 5 balls. In first-class cricket he took 571 wickets in a career which lasted for twenty-five years. He also scored 18,212 runs, and made 335 catches in 283 matches, mostly at slip where he excelled.

Peter Pollock (*right*) was one of the most brilliant fast bowlers that South Africa has ever produced. He played for Eastern Province, with his brother Graeme, from 1958 to 1972 and opened the bowling for South Africa in twenty-eight Test matches in which he took 116 wickets. Playing nearly all of his cricket in South Africa, he was restricted to 127 matches in his first-class career, yet he took 485 wickets in that time. Strong and hostile, he made his first-class debut at the age of seventeen and took 9 wickets in his first Test match at the age of twenty. He was a batsman good enough to average 22.59 in his career.

Two Great Left-handers

Graeme Pollock (seen right, with Alan Knott keeping wicket) is still scoring centuries for Transvaal and is now nearing 20,000 runs at an average of 55. In twenty-three Test matches he scored 2,256 runs, average 60.97, and as, apart from his Test tours, all his cricket has been in the South African domestic seasons where he has four times passed 1,000 runs, his achievements are remarkable. It is not simply the number of runs that Pollock has scored, but the manner in which he has scored them. He is always attacking the bowling, always technically sound and, above all, always aesthetically pleasing.

Described by many as the world's greatest cricketer in the post-war period, Gary Sobers, seen left in typically flowing, aggressive style, became the first batsman to reach 8,000 runs in Test cricket. He ended with 8,032, including the record 365 not out for the West Indies against Pakistan, 1957–8, and as he also took 235 Test wickets and made 109 catches, the claim that he is the best all-round cricketer the world has seen is not an exaggerated one. In his ninety-three Tests for the West Indies he was captain thirty-nine times.

He played for Barbados, South Australia and Nottinghamshire. He could bowl left-arm medium or slow, and to watch him bat was to be excited. His career brought him 28,315 runs and 1,043 wickets as well as 407 catches.

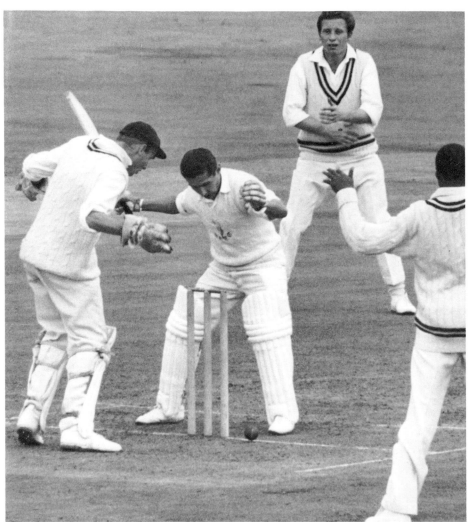

A. C. Smith

Alan Smith was a most popular captain of Oxford University and led the side in 1959 and 1960. He had made his debut for Warwickshire in 1958, the year he won his first blue, and he was to play for them for the next sixteen years. A middle-order batsman and good wicket-keeper who also did the hat-trick against Essex with his seamers, Smith captained Warwickshire from 1968 until his retirement in 1974. He is now county secretary and has managed England touring sides. He was captain of Warwickshire when they won the County Championship in 1972.

On the left, he looks in wonder as a ball from Bob Barber evades batsman Alan Rees of Glamorgan but does not break the wicket. Alan Gordon is the fielder and Lance Gibbs throws his arms in anticipation. Rees played rugby for Wales and later joined Leeds Rugby League Club.

In the same season, 1968, Smith (*below*) catches Doug Padgett of Yorkshire off the bowling of Tom Cartwright for 2. Padgett wheels away without waiting for the umpire's decision. Kanhai, finger raised in appeal, and Gibbs are the slip fielders. Warwickshire went on to beat Yorkshire by 165 runs. This catch provided Cartwright with one of his seven wickets in the first Yorkshire innings.

John Sydney Buller

The saddest picture in Ken Kelly's folio. It is 7 August 1970, at Edgbaston, the third day of the County Championship match between Warwickshire and Nottinghamshire. Rain has brought the players off the field in the middle of the Warwickshire second innings. It has never been customary to take photographs in such circumstances, but some instinct prompted Ken Kelly to take a picture of umpire Syd Buller as he left the field in conversation with David Halfyard, followed by Dennis Amiss and Garfield Sobers. A few moments later Buller collapsed and died in the pavilion.

Kelly played cricket with Buller's nephew in the Wyther Park Council School team in Leeds and Syd Buller coached the side on occasions, Kelly's first meeting with Buller. When Ken Kelly moved to the Midlands he again contacted Syd Buller and the two became firm friends. He is still unaware of what impulse made him photograph Buller on what was seemingly a trivial occasion but transpired to be a tragic one, for Buller was never seen again before the cricketing public after this moment.

Buller played one match for his native Yorkshire in 1930. He knew that with Arthur Wood as the regular wicket-keeper his chances with Yorkshire were limited, so he joined Worcestershire in 1935.

Tragedy came into Buller's life on 28 May 1939, a Whit Sunday rest day in a match against Essex at Chelmsford. He was badly injured in a car crash in which his team mate Charlie Bull was killed. It was early August before Buller played again, and as World War II started in September 1939, he did not play for Worcestershire again until 1946.

Although Buller's playing career spanned the years between 1930 and 1946, his years in the wilderness with Yorkshire, and the loss of six war years while with Worcestershire, meant that he only played in 112 first-class matches. In these games he had 249 wicket-keeper victims, 178 caught and 71 stumped, and he scored 1,746 runs at an average of 13.74.

Season 1947 saw him as the Worcestershire coach, and in 1951 he joined the First Class Umpires List. Syd Buller was one of the finest umpires ever to have stood in a Test match and he was awarded the MBE for his services to cricket. He umpired in thirty-three Test matches between 1956 and 1969, and was known as a fair-minded man who was honest in his opinions and completely dedicated to the game. He took a leading part in the elimination of 'throwing', notably when he no-balled South African Griffin in 1960.

Tom Graveney

After twelve years with Gloucestershire Tom Graveney moved to Worcestershire, and he spent the last nine years of his cricketing life there.

Fate took Graveney to Worcester; his elegant and stylish batting fitted into the overall scene at the New Road ground. To watch Graveney batting with the sun glinting on the cathedral, its chimes and bells ringing, was a scene of cricket perfection.

Graveney matured, as a person and as a

batsman at Worcestershire, and he played his part in the two County Championship winning teams of 1964 and 1965 (their centenary year). In ten seasons at Worcestershire, he scored 13,160 runs at an average of 46.02, so his adopted county had sterling service from this most prolific craftsman of his generation. Many a batsman received inspiration and advice from Graveney, none more than Glenn Turner, who went on to break many of the Worcestershire batting records in the seventies. His cover drive, pictured below, brought memories of Wally Hammond

Left Tom Graveney hitting a six, again with style and no hint of violence

Turner and Graveney

For his last two years at Worcester Tom Graveney was joined by the New Zealander Glenn Turner. Turner (*right*) hit ten centuries for Worcestershire in 1970, Graveney's last season, and established a new county record. On 3 September, Turner and Graveney (*far right*) shared a stand of 124 against Warwickshire. Both batsmen are pictured during that stand, which was in Graveney's last match for the county, and Billy Ibadulla is the fielder. Graveney predicted that Turner would be the batsman of the seventies and he was right, as all statistics prove

Below Tom Graveney is applauded from the field by his fellow cricketers from Worcestershire and Warwickshire and, appropriately backed by the beauty of Worcester Cathedral, he leaves the first-class cricket field for the last time

The stand was ended next morning. It had produced 291 in 5 hours, 51 minutes. It established a new Pakistan second wicket record in first-class cricket. Mushtaq Mohammad, pictured below with Alan Knott behind the stumps and Colin Cowdrey at first slip, was caught by Cowdrey off Illingworth for exactly 100. Zaheer's innings lasted 9 hours, 10 minutes and he scored 274, the first double century hit by a Pakistani against England. On the opposite page, he is seen driving one of his thirty-eight fours. Again, Knott and Cowdrey keep a watchful eye. During the course of his innings, which established him as one of the world's great players, Zaheer became the first batsman in the English season to reach a thousand runs. Above, he is escorted from the field by adoring fans, some of whom appear to be West Indian, the first time such an incident occurred in a Test match in England.

Asif Iqbal, Alan Knott and Brian Luckhurst also scored centuries in the Test match at Edgbaston which England drew, play ending early through rain after they had been forced to follow-on.

In 1972 Zaheer Abbas joined Gloucestershire and remained a firm favourite with them until he retired from county cricket at the end of 1984.

Zaheer Abbas

Although he had averaged 93.00 in the leading domestic competition in Pakistan, the Qaid-e-Azam Trophy, at the age of nineteen, Zaheer Abbas' Test debut did not come until October 1969, when, at the age of twenty-two, he scored 12 and 27 against New Zealand in Karachi. He did not play in the rest of the series, but he was chosen for the tour of England in 1971. The first Test match was played at Edgbaston and Zaheer found himself at the wicket to face the fourth ball of the innings on the first day after Aftab Gul had been stuck on the head by Ward's third delivery and forced to retire hurt. Zaheer and Sadiq took the score to 68 before Sadiq fell to Peter Lever. Zaheer was joined by Mushtaq Mohammad and by the end of the first day Pakistan were 270 for 1. The pair had added 82 in the last session of the day and the crowd had been thrilled by some brilliant batting, Zaheer's exciting stroke play piercing the field with ease.

Gleeson and Inverarity

John Gleeson was one of the Australian 'mystery' bowlers. He could spin the ball both ways at a brisk pace and took 430 first-class wickets although he did not make his debut until he was twenty-eight. Seen here in action (*left*), with John Langridge umpiring, he propelled the ball off a bent middle finger as another Australian 'mystery' bowler, Jack Iverson, had done. He did well in England in 1968 and in South Africa two years later, but thereafter he declined and in England in 1972 took only 3 wickets in three Tests. Nevertheless he finished with 93 wickets from his twenty-nine Tests. His weakness was that, in an effort to produce a variety, he bowled many loose deliveries which were punished. John Inverarity (*below*), whose career began before Gleeson's and went on eleven years after Gleeson had retired, leaps to catch Alan Smith at Edgbaston in 1968. The bowler was Renneberg. John Inverarity retired from first-class cricket in March 1985, after twenty-three years in the game. He was an outstanding leader of men and following triumphs with Western Australia he moved to South Australia where he inspired more success and to the end continued to take wickets with his slow left-arm. In 1984 he passed Bradman's record to become the most prolific scorer in the Sheffield Shield.

John William Gleeson
Career bowling: 1,117 matches, 430 wickets at 24.95
Test bowling: 29 matches, 93 wickets at 36.20

Robert John Inverarity
Career matches: 203 matches, 10,995 runs at 36.16, 160 wickets at 30.45
Test matches: 6 matches, 174 runs at 17.40, 4 wickets at 23.25

Three Australian Stalwarts

Doug Walters (*right*) was something of a disappointment in England although he came here four times with the Australian side and was unlucky not to be selected for a fifth tour in 1981. He was a tremendously popular batsman in Australia and his attacking style was a delight. He played in seventy-four Tests and scored 5,357 runs at an average of 48.26. He was a more than useful medium-pace bowler. Ross Edwards (*below left*) was a less flamboyant, but equally likeable, middle-order batsman who played in twenty Tests. He excelled in the field and became particularly renowned for his work in the covers.

Keith Stackpole (*below right*) was an exciting opening batsman who attacked the bowling right from the start. He played in forty-three Test matches, but he came only once to England, in 1972, when he was vice-captain. In Test matches on this tour he made more runs than anyone else on either side. He was a useful leg-break bowler and a fine close-to-the-wicket fielder. Since his retirement he has become one of Australia's leading television commentators.

Kevin Douglas Walters

Career matches: 258 matches, 16, 180 runs at 43.84, 190 wickets at 35.69

Test matches: 74 matches, 5,357 runs at 48.26, 49 wickets at 29.08

Ross Edwards

Career batting: 126 matches, 7,345 runs at 39.27

Test batting: 20 matches, 1,171 runs at 40.37

Keith Raymond Stackpole

Career batting: 167 matches, 10,100 runs at 39.29

Test batting: 43 matches, 2,807 runs at 37.42

The Howarth Brothers

New Zealand's main attacking weapon in the 1970s was the slow left-arm bowling of Hedley Howarth. He made his Test debut against England at Lord's in 1969 and took the first five of his 86 Test wickets. In all, he was to play in thirty Tests. In first-class cricket he took 541 wickets, a total bettered only by Richard Hadlee among New Zealand bowlers.

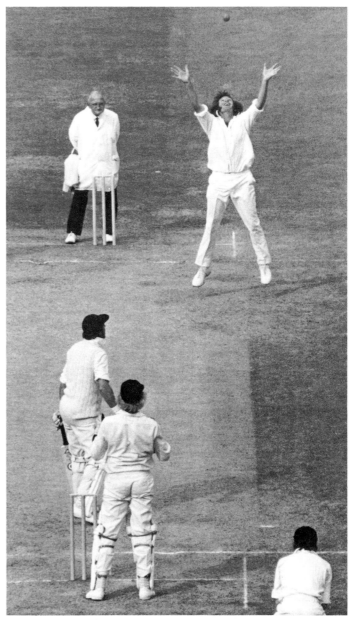

Hedley Howarth retired in 1979, but the family tradition was continued by his younger brother Geoff who made his Test debut in 1975. Geoff Howarth, pictured above, served an apprenticeship with Surrey, whom he now captains, before establishing himself in New Zealand. A tenacious and hard-working batsman, he has become an outstanding captain, leading New Zealand to Test victories over every Test-playing country, and to their first Test win in England. He has become a national hero, associated as he is with the golden age of New Zealand cricket.

Right Geoff Boycott becomes one of Hedley Howarth's Test victims. Howarth throws the ball in the air with delight after accepting a return catch from the Yorkshireman at Lord's, June 1973. Wadsworth is the wicket-keeper and Tom Spencer is the umpire

Above Vic Pollard of New Zealand on the way to a century at Trent Bridge, 1973. He headed the Test batting averages on this tour, 302 runs at an average 100.66

Right Richard Hadlee bowling, 1978

Below Tavaré bowled by Ewen Chatfield in 1983 at Headingley during New Zealand's first Test victory in England

Above left Alan Jones of Glamorgan in the 1977 Gillette Cup Final at Lord's. He scored a thousand runs in twenty-three seasons. Perhaps England's best uncapped post-war batsman, he has scored more runs in first-class cricket than any other non-test player, 36,049 at an average 32.89

Above Geoff Boycott during his ninety-eighth century at Trent Bridge in 1977

Derek Underwood at Trent Bridge in 1977. 'Dickie' Bird is the umpire, Bob Woolmer the fielder

John Snow

The son of a Sussex vicar, John Snow was the most aggressive, and unquestionably among the most talented of England fast bowlers in the post-war period. He joined Sussex as a batsman and remained a useful batsman to the end of his career, making his maiden fifty in first-class cricket in The Oval Test match against the West Indies in 1966 when he and Higgs added 128 in 140 minutes for the last wicket, only two runs short of the England record. After his retirement from Sussex in 1977, he returned to play Sunday League cricket for Warwickshire for a time.

Tall and wiry, with an easy rhythm and a relaxed stride, he delivered the ball with intelligence and intensity and had a fine follow-through, as seen in the picture on the right. He made his first-class debut in 1961 and first played for England in 1965, and took four wickets in each of his two Tests, against New Zealand and South Africa. He had the reputation of not being easy to handle and his 'rebelliousness' led to suspension after he had barged into Gavaskar when the batsman was taking a quick single in the Lord's Test match of 1971. By then Snow was established as an England hero, his fiery temperament fitting the public image of what a fast bowler should be. In 1967–8, he had played a vital part in England's victory in the West Indies. He took 7 for 49 in the second Test in Jamaica as the West Indies were shot out for 143, Snow having Sobers lbw first ball. In the third Test, he took 5 for 86 and 3 for 39, and 4 for 82 and 6 for 60 in the last Test. This meant that in only four Tests he had established an England record against the West Indies with 27 wickets.

When England regained the Ashes under Illingworth in 1970–1, Snow was the leading strike weapon, taking 31 wickets in the series at 22.83. He also averaged 23.50 with the bat. It should be remembered, too, that not one Australian batsman was adjudged lbw in the entire series.

When Australia came to England in 1972 and drew the series 2–2, Snow was again the leading fast bowler. The picture below shows Peter Parfitt taking a fine low catch at second slip to dismiss Bob Massie at Trent Bridge in the third Test. This catch gave John Snow his fifth wicket of the innings.

He played for England until 1976, when he was thirty-five, although he was never selected for a tour after the 1970–1 series.

In his forty-nine Test matches Snow took 202 wickets at 26.66 each, and in all first-class cricket took 1,174 wickets at a cost of 22.72 runs each.

Ray Illingworth

Ray Illingworth first played for Yorkshire in 1951. He was a capable all-rounder, a solid batsman, an accurate off-spinner and an excellent fielder, particularly in the gully. Between 1951 and 1968 he scored over 14,000 runs and took nearly 1,400 wickets for Yorkshire. He scored fourteen centuries for the county and three times he did the 'double'.

On the left, he is seen bowling his off-spin in the Headingley Test match against the Australians in 1972. He took 4 wickets in the match and played an important part in England's victory by 9 wickets. Greg Chappell is the Australian batsman and 'Dusty' Rhodes is the umpire.

Below In the same match, Illingworth displays his excellence as a fielder. He has pivoted and is falling backwards as he takes the ball in his right hand to dismiss Paul Sheahan off the bowling of Derek Underwood for 0. It was one of three catches that Illingworth took in the innings and he was a great help to Underwood who had match figures of 10 for 82. Alan Knott is the wicket-keeper and Peter Parfitt is at slip

At the end of 1968 Illingworth left Yorkshire and was appointed captain of Leicestershire for the 1969 season. He was thirty-seven years old and had played in thirty Test matches, with no great success, over a period of thirteen series. His influence on Leicestershire was immediate. In ten years under his captaincy they won five major trophies, including the County Championship in 1975.

Illingworth, seen right batting in his Leicestershire sweater, added a new dimension to the side and the England selectors quickly recognised his qualities of leadership. An injury to Colin Cowdrey, the England captain, resulted in the selectors turning to Illingworth and he was envisaged as a caretaker captain until Cowdrey returned to fitness. He first led England against the West Indies at Old Trafford and England won there for the first time in ten years. The second Test at Lord's was drawn, but Illingworth, going in at 189 for 6, hit a maiden Test hundred and was established as a national hero. His popularity became even greater when England won the third and final Test and below he is seen signing bats in the England dressing-room with David Brown, the Warwickshire fast bowler who took 14 wickets in the three Tests. Greater honour was in store for Illingworth for, in 1970–1, England regained the Ashes when he led the side to Australia.

In 1973 he was awarded the CBE for his services to cricket and he was to captain his country in thirty-one Test matches. He returned to Yorkshire as manager in 1979 and captained the ailing side in 1982 at the age of fifty. He led them to a John Player Special League triumph in 1983, but he left them the following year, a victim of the divisions within the county over the future of Boycott.

Raymond Illingworth

Career matches: 672 matches, 24, 134 runs at 28.06, 2,072 wickets at 20.28 runs each

Test matches: 61 matches, 1,836 runs at 23.24, 122 wickets at 31.20 runs each

Bomb Scare at Lord's

In August 1973, when an IRA bomb campaign was prevalent in London, a telephone call was received at Lord's on the Saturday of the third Test match between England and the West Indies saying that a bomb had been planted in the stands. The authorities had no option but to treat the call seriously, even though it later proved to be a hoax, and 28,000 people were ordered to leave the ground. In fact, the majority surged onto the playing area to produce one of the most remarkable scenes ever witnessed at the famous ground.

The picture on the left shows the crowd mingling and chatting on the pitch while the police search the stands. The incident caused the loss of eighty-five minutes play and it was agreed to continue until 7.00pm on the Saturday and to extend play on the Monday and Tuesday. This proved not to be necessary as the West Indies won with a day and a half to spare.

Right Umpire Dickie Bird sits on the covers jealously guarding the wicket as the crowd swarm round him. No damage was done to the playing surface and there was much good humour between umpire and spectators

Rohan Kanhai and the Bottle of Champagne

The West Indies win the match and the series against England at Lord's in 1973. They won by an innings and 226 runs, with Kanhai, Sobers and Julien scoring centuries and Gibbs taking 5 wickets for 65 runs in the match. The captain of the West Indies, Rohan Kanhai, appeared on the dressing-room balcony after the match in response to the cheers of the crowd. His West Indies supporters had given such devoted support and encouragement to his team that Kanhai, as a token of his gratitude, dropped a bottle of champagne into the crowd so they could also join in the celebrations.

In the first picture Kanhai drops the bottle, watched by Deryck Murray, and in the second picture hands close over the bottle and the struggle is on for the honour of the first drink. The third picture shows the 'big fella', who alternates between blowing his bugle and playing the bongo drums, in possession, and about to open the bottle. As it opens, the spray showers both the crowd and the police who all take it in good heart, and the last picture shows the sweet taste of success as the celebrations begin.

Mike Smith

Mike Smith, all-round sportsman and popular captain of England and Warwickshire, was a right-handed batsman who combined sound defence with an attractive range of strokes. *Left* He plays a fine off-drive against Pakistan. Wicket-keeper Wasim Bari, the finest ever produced by Pakistan, crouches behind the stumps. It was said by many critics, that Mike Smith was just an on-side player, but as this picture proves he could drive straight or through the off-side with great timing and power.

Smith retired from playing cricket in 1967, but came back into the game in 1970. When he finally retired, at the end of season 1975, he had played in three more Tests against Australia, in 1972, and also helped Warwickshire to win the County Championship title the same year.

He hit sixty-nine centuries in his career, and was as valuable a fielder as he was a batsman. He holds two Warwickshire fielding records: six catches in an innings against Leicestershire at Hinckley in 1962 and 422 in his career with the county. In all matches he held 592 catches.

Michael John Knight Smith

Career batting: 637 matches, 39,832 runs at 41.84
Test batting: 50 matches, 2,278 runs at 31.63

Below Smith flings himself to his left to catch Boycott off David Brown. It was Warwickshire's first home game of the 1973 season and it was ruined by rain. Warwickshire had won the title the previous season and their wealth of talent can be seen in this picture; from left to right their other players are Bob Willis, Dennis Amiss, John Jameson, Rohan Kanhai and Deryck Murray, the West Indian wicket-keeper. The six Warwickshire players in this photograph won nearly 350 Test caps between them and three of them, Mike Smith, Rohan Kanhai and Bob Willis, captained their countries

Bob Willis the Destroyer

There is no greater sight in cricket than the fast bowler sending the stumps cartwheeling.

Above A Bob Willis hat-trick, all bowled, Warwickshire *v* Yorkshire John Player League match, Edgbaston, 17 June 1973. First, Richard Hutton swings wildly and has his middle stump knocked out of the ground. Second, David Bairstow chops down too late on a ball that moves into him and is bowled leg-stump. Third, Phil Carrick drives lazily at a straight ball and his middle stump is knocked back. Woodford surveys all in amazement

Right Deryck Murray swings and his middle stump goes out of the ground. England *v* West Indies at Trent Bridge, 1980. Murray had scored 64

Below Farokh Engineer is an earlier Willis Test victim, England *v* India, first Test match at Old Trafford, June 1974. Willis beats Engineer's forward shot and knocks a stump out of the ground. The batsman had not scored and England went on to win the match

Award Winning Picture

Ron Headley, the Worcestershire and West Indies opening batsman, loses his bat in the Gillette Cup semi-final against Gloucestershire, at Worcester, August 1973. Bat, ball and a slice of rubber
from the bat handle fly away to the bewilderment of Headley.

Ken Kelly's picture, taken with a 600mm lens, was named as
Sports Picture of the Year in the Sports Photographer of the Year
competition, sponsored by the Sports Council and the Royal
Photographic Society of Great Britain. With the picture, entitled
Knock-out Cricket, in the background, Kelly receives his award
from Dr Roger Bannister, CBE, the Chairman of the Sports Council.

Dr Bannister later learned from Kelly that he was one of the four
photographers present at Iffley Road, Oxford, in 1954, when
Bannister became the first man to break the four-minute mile
barrier, a link between a great achievement and that present award
which Dr Bannister was delighted to bring to the attention of the
audience.

Above Vivian Richards, 1981

Right Clive Lloyd, The Oval, 1976

Alvin Kallicharan turns a ball past Gatting, 1980, at Lord's

Headingley, Leeds, during the parched summer of 1984, England vs
West Indies

Edgbaston, Birmingham, England vs West Indies, 1984

Queen's Park, Chesterfield, Derbyshire, 1976, with the famous crooked spire in the background

Old Trafford, Manchester. The first Sunday play in a Test Match, England vs Australia, 1981. Note the photographers

Lord's, Jubilee Test 1977, England vs Australia

Imran Khan bowling, with Gower the non-striker and Zaheer Abbas the fielder. England vs Pakistan at Lord's, 1982

Amal Silva of Sri Lanka during his century
at Lord's, 1984

Trent Bridge, Nottingham, 1980, England vs West Indies

The Oval, London, 1977, England vs Australia

Melbourne: Australia vs West Indies, 1975

Right Melbourne: Australia vs West Indies, 1975

Sydney: Australia vs West Indies, 1976

Left Greg Chappell batting at Sydney, 1976

Above Jeff Thomson bowling to Roy Fredericks at Melbourne, 1975

Rodney Marsh breaks the wicket at Sydney, 1976

Indian Heroes

Sunil Gavaskar (*right*), the greatest of Indian batsmen, who now holds the record number of thirty centuries in Test cricket. In the picture he is on his way to one of his Test hundreds, 101 *v* England at Old Trafford in 1974, an innings which he considered his best

Below A fine all-round cricketer, Madan Lal, is dismissed in a most peculiar manner in the same match. Mike Hendrick on his Test debut has bowled Madan Lal and the batsman looks back to see off and leg stump knocked out of the ground and middle stump left standing. Obviously, he is puzzled. The ball had moved in very late from the off, hit the off stump and knocked it back, clipped the middle, disturbing it only fractionally, before crashing into the leg stump and knocking it out of the ground

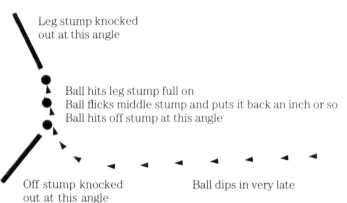

Leg stump knocked out at this angle

Ball hits leg stump full on
Ball flicks middle stump and puts it back an inch or so
Ball hits off stump at this angle

Off stump knocked out at this angle

Ball dips in very late

Garfield Sobers

Gary Sobers is unquestionably the greatest all-rounder that cricket has ever known. He began as a slow left-arm bowler who was also a useful batsman, and it was in this capacity that he made his Test debut against England in March 1954. He was seventeen years old and took 4 for 75 in an innings of 414. He quickly added the chinaman and googly to his repertoire and was readily accepted as a top-line spinner, as he demonstrates in the picture below. Playing for South Australia in the Sheffield Shield between 1961 and 1964, he extended his bowling to include fast medium and within a short time had become the most deadly new-ball bowler in the world, often opening the West Indian attack ahead of Wes Hall or Charlie Griffith. It became common for him to use his three different styles of bowling in one session of play, and all were equally effective.

As a young man, he was fast and agile anywhere in the field, but as he grew older he concentrated on fielding close to the wicket where his quick reactions and ability to pluck catches out of mid-air put his fielding on a par with his other qualities and brought him 109 catches in ninety-three Test matches.

On the left, Sobers is shown in the delivery stride as a seam bowler. At Headingley in 1963 he scored 102 and 52 and then opened the West Indies bowling in the second innings to bowl Stewart without a run on the board and set up the West Indies first victory at Leeds.

Right Gary Sobers at full stretch
Below Sobers the fielder. He throws the ball in the air after catching Ray Illingworth, the England captain, at backward short-leg off the bowling of Lance Gibbs in the Lord's Test of 1973. It was one of six catches he took in the match in which he also scored 150 not out

As quickly as Sobers' bowling developed in versatility, so his batting increased in stature and within four years of his first Test match for the West Indies he hit the record Test score of 365 not out against Pakistan. He had command of all the shots. He cut hard and viciously (*left*) so that the ball sped to the boundary from the bat and never offered the fielder a moment of hope that he would stop it. He had a generous pick-up and a long follow-through which made his driving straight and on the off-side one of the great delights of the modern game. Off the back foot or (*right*) off the front foot, there was a beauty and majesty in the drive which drew gasps of admiration from the crowd. His ability was apparent wherever he played, and for South Australia in 1963–4 he scored more than a thousand runs and took over fifty wickets, a feat unique in Australian cricket. In 1971–2, he hit 254 for the Rest of the World against Australia, an innings which Sir Donald Bradman described as the most magnificent and masterly he had ever seen in a representative match. It was not just the number of runs that he scored that determined Sobers' quality, but the manner in which he scored them. When he beat Hutton's record, for example, he scored his runs in three hours less time than Hutton had done at The Oval in 1938 and hit thirty-eight fours.

A great cutter and driver of the ball, as shown in the pictures above, Sobers was a magnificent hitter on the up as we can see from the picture on the right. He played for Nottinghamshire between 1968 and 1974 and led the county in an exciting manner. In his first season with the county, in the game against Glamorgan at Swansea, he hit Malcolm Nash, who was bowling slow left-arm, for six sixes in an over, a feat which remained unchallented until Ravi Shashtri equalled it in 1985. Born in Barbados, whom he led to triumphs in the Shell Shield, Sobers succeeded Frank Worrell as captain of the West Indies and led them in thirty-nine Tests, which was then a record. Towards the end of his career he was troubled by a knee injury and he was forced to retire in 1974. A year later he was knighted for his services to cricket and by this time he had become to many people the best cricketer that they had ever seen.

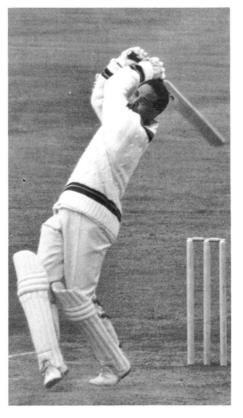

Sir Garfield St Auburn Sobers
Born Bridgetown, Barbados, 28 July 1936
Career batting: 383 matches, 609 innings, 93 times not out, 28,315 runs, highest score 365 not out, average 54.87, 86 centuries
Test batting: 93 Tests, 160 innings, 21 times not out, 8,032 runs, highest score 365 not out, average 57.78, 26 centuries
Career bowling: 1,043 wickets for 28,941 runs, average 27.74, best bowling 9 for 49 (West Indies *v* Kent, 1966)
Test bowling: 235 wickets for 7,999 runs, average 34.03, best bowling 6 for 73
Catches: (career) 407; (Test) 109

Mike Procter

He joined Gloucestershire in 1965 and played for them until 1981, when he was forced to give up county cricket because of a knee injury, although he continued to play for Natal for another three years. He captained Gloucestershire from 1977 to 1981 and few men have done as much for a county. Throughout his career he was a dynamic cricketer and his enthusiastic approach to the game was infectious. It is one of the tragedies of the South African situation that Procter had played only seven Test matches before his country was exiled from international cricket. He was a very quick bowler, with an unusual action. He also bowled off-breaks when the occasion demanded and took 1,407 wickets in his career to complement his 21,904 runs. In 1970–1 he hit six hundreds in six consecutive innings for Rhodesia.

He was such a force at Gloucestershire that for a time in the seventies the county was nicknamed 'Proctershire'. He joined the World Series Cricket of Kerry Packer and once again demonstrated his talent at international level.

Procter was a violent, but accurate, hitter of the ball, as can be seen here where, in pre-Packer days without a helmet, he executes the cover drive

The picture above shows that, despite common belief, Procter did not bowl off the wrong foot. It was his fast, whippy arm action, and the weight projected forward, that gave the 'wrong foot' impression. Fred Jakeman is the umpire

His commitment to Gloucestershire was total and he was immensely popular with players and spectators. He even found it possible to survive the English weather and (*above left*) having just returned from Durban, he reads a book on Viv Richards in the dressing-room as the rain beats down during the opening match of the 1980 season

Above Gloucestershire's day of glory. Procter is held aloft by his team-mates and he holds the Benson and Hedges Cup under his arm after Gloucestershire had beaten Kent in the 1977 Final at Lord's. The Gloucestershire players pause in their own celebrations to applaud their opponents who are just collecting their losers' medals

Michael John Procter
Career matches: 393 matches, 21,748 runs at 36.24, 1,395 wickets at 19.19
Test matches: 7 matches, 226 runs at 25.11, 41 wickets at 15.02

Procter made as great an impact on English cricket at Gloucestershire as Eddie Barlow did at Derbyshire. Here he chats with two other overseas players who have made a significant impact on English cricket, Clive Lloyd at Lancashire and Viv Richards at Somerset. The occasion is the Gloucestershire-West Indies match in 1980

South Africa last played Test cricket in 1970 and so a generation of outstanding cricketers was denied international experience. To develop their talents and display them on a broader stage some sought to play for English counties and they have enriched first-class cricket in this country.

Clive Rice, pictured left bowling his medium pacers with Dickie Bird as umpire, joined Nottinghamshire in 1975 and became captain of the county in 1979. Under his leadership Notts won the County Championship in 1981 and finished as runners-up in 1984. Although injury has hampered his bowling, Rice has continued as a prolific scorer. He has also led the all-conquering Transvaal team in domestic competitions in South Africa and became captain of the unofficial Test side in 1984.

Eddie Barlow had the advantage of playing thirty Test matches before South Africa's exile and he is now a leading negotiator in the country's efforts to return to international cricket. A splendid all-round cricketer, he took over as captain of an ailing Derbyshire side in 1976 and led them for nearly three seasons, instilling a sense of purpose and commitment and lifting the team by his own efforts. He maintained an infectious zest for the game and was forty-four when he retired from first-class cricket. The impression he made upon cricket in Derbyshire was an indelible one and the NatWest Cup Final win in 1981 was a tribute to the legacy that he left

Ken McEwan hit 99 as captain of South African Schools and was hailed as his country's new batting hero. Three months later South Africa was banned from Test cricket and McEwan became the first of a lost generation. In 1974 he joined Essex and his rise has coincided with the rise of Essex to eminence in English cricket. A batsman of classical elegance who has delighted crowds throughout England, McEwan joined Gooch in a memorable second wicket partnership when Essex won the Benson and Hedges Cup in 1979, and, in 1983, he was the first player in the country to reach 1,000 runs and the first to 2,000 runs as well. He has scored 1,000 runs in every year he has played cricket in England, and rarely have they been anything but exciting and entertaining to watch as the drive for six over mid-wicket pictured right typifies. He and Barry Richards (*below*) are the only players to have been in Sheffield Shield, Currie Cup and County Championship winning sides: McEwan with Western Australia, Western Province and Essex; Richards with South Australia, Natal and Hampshire.

Barry Richards clips the ball to leg. He had over 28,000 runs to his credit and hit two centuries in the four Test matches in which he was able to play. An opening batsman of complete authority and eagerness to attack, he was the lost master of the 1970s and one can only surmise what records he would have broken had he been permitted a full Test career

Bishen Bedi

One of the great pictures of a spin bowler in action, and one that has been used frequently. Ken Kelly studied Bedi's action from several angles and, having photographed the bowler several times, examined the results and discovered at what point in the action he would get the most satisfying picture. He has encapsulated the concentration and the grace of the great spinner. Kelly's study took some three to four years, but the end product was a definitive picture of an outstanding player which gave the artist a deep sense of satisfaction for it was the culmination of an artistic process. Bedi served Northamptonshire well and took 266 Test wickets

One of Bedi's Test wickets: Dennis Amiss is taken at slip by Sunil Gavaskar for 47. Farokh Engineer is the wicket-keeper, Solkar the fielder, David Constant the umpire, and the occasion is the second innings of the Old Trafford Test of 1974

'Venkat' bowling at The Oval in 1979, England vs India

Gower caught by wicket-keeper Reddy bowled Bedi, The Oval, 1979, England vs India

Graham Yallop scores a century in 1981 at Old Trafford vs England

John Emburey bowls to a spinner's field at The Oval, 1981, England vs Australia

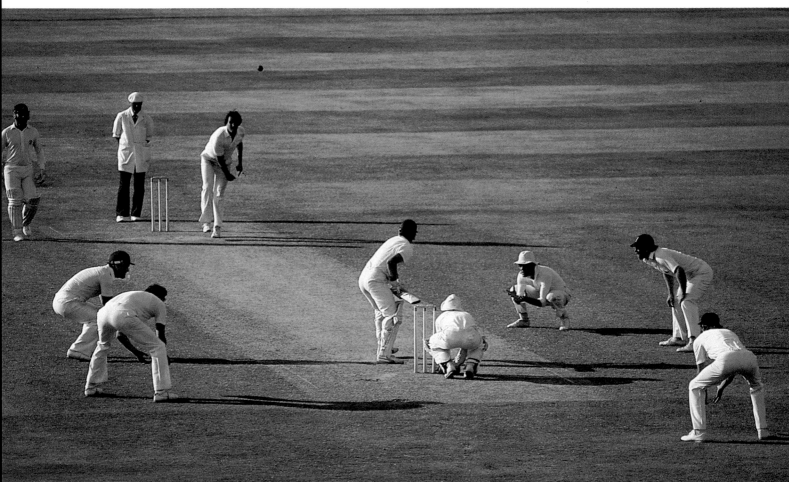

Controversy

The Pakistan touring side lodged an official complaint accusing the MCC of incompetence in covering the pitch after rain had leaked under the covers overnight during the Lord's Test between England and Pakistan in 1974. The covers had been lifted by the wind, and when the wicket was inspected in the morning it was apparent that it had become an ideal surface for the bowling of Derek Underwood. One patch was on a perfect length and Underwood took 5 for 20 and 8 for 51. Rain on the last day denied England victory and many felt that justice had been done.

Intikhab Alam, the Pakistan captain, inspects the pitch with England skipper Mike Denness, umpire David Constant and Asif Iqbal. Mushtaq Mohammad takes photographs of the offending wicket

Below Intikhab falls to Underwood twice in the match. In the first innings he loses his leg bail, and in the second innings his leg stump. On both occasions he was bowled round his legs. The liberal sprinklings of sand at the pitch edges show the state of the surface and the difficulties that the Pakistanis encountered

111

Unusual Pictures
Keith Fletcher enjoys a lucky escape while batting for England at Headingley in 1974. He edges to slip where Majid Khan and Shafiq Ahmed both go for the ball. The ball eludes them, but Majid appears to have caught Shafiq on the nose. It was Shafiq Ahmed's Test debut

A bizarre picture: Phil Edmonds dives and Peter Johnson runs for the same crease, as Deryck Murray breaks the wicket to run both of them out. Johnson, later to play for Nottinghamshire, was the player who walked. Edmonds, of course, later played for Middlesex and England although here, like Johnson, he is playing for Cambridge University against the University Athletic Union in the Courtauld Trophy Final of 1971. Murray, the West Indian Test keeper, was a student at Nottingham University

The Prudential World Cup Semi-Final, Headingley, 1975, saw England bowled out for 93, with Gary Gilmour taking 6 for 14. Australia were reduced to 39 for 6 in reply, and at that point Gilmour joined Doug Walters and steered Australia to victory. Gilmour should have been run out in this incident when Walters sent him back and he dived for the crease as Frank Hayes, looking dejected, shied at the wicket and missed. (Left to right) Walters, Gilmour in a heap, Hayes, Greig (arms folded), Denness (who has prevented an over-throw), Wood, Fletcher (hands on head), Snow (head down), Peter Lever (hands on head) and Knott (arms raised)

Bob Woolmer seems to have lost his head as Ian Chappell sweeps. The ball went off Woolmer's body to the boundary. John Edrich and Alan Knott look to see if Woolmer's head is still on his shoulders. England *v* Australia at Lord's, 1975

Dennis Amiss
He joined Warwickshire in 1958 straight from school, so he has spent a life-time with the county. A modest and charming man, he enjoys his pipe (*right*) while proudly wearing his England blazer and tie. He has played in fifty Tests and has scored 3,612 runs, including two double centuries agaisnt the West Indies.

Amiss hits out during his innings of 96 against Pakistan at Edgbaston in 1971. He and Mike Smith added 162 in just over two hours for Warwickshire against the tourists

He square cuts a boundary during his innings of 203 against the West Indies at The Oval in 1976, a valiant knock when the rest of the England side was falling to Holding

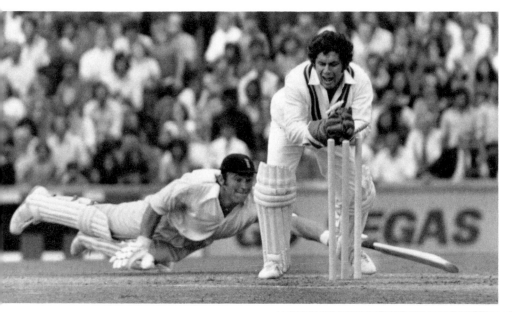

Amiss gets the benefit of the doubt after diving home as Wasim Bari breaks the wicket at The Oval, 1974. Taken without a motor-wind, this picture demanded precision timing if the moment was to be captured. Amiss went on to make 183. Umpire Dickie Bird later said that the television replay made him think Amiss may have been out

Amiss sways to avoid a Jeff Thomson bouncer at Old Trafford, 1974. Amiss was 'bounced' out of Test cricket and was one of the first to advocate the wearing of helmets; he actually designed his own, initially using motor-cycle helmets

Even with a helmet Amiss is a target for fast bowler Wayne Daniel, but, at the age of forty-two, he remains the most technically accomplished batsman in England and he is now within reach of joining the elite band of batsmen who have scored a hundred hundreds. Originally an opening batsman, he has now dropped to number 4, and there is no batsman in the country who gives greater aesthetic pleasure

Spinners

In an age and a country dominated by pace, Lance Gibbs still remained supreme with his off-spin. He took 309 wickets in his seventy-nine Tests for the West Indies, and 1,024 in the whole of his first-class career. He played for British Guiana (now Guyana), Warwickshire and South Australia.

Below left A great off-spinner of a different type is Jack Simmons of Lancashire. He bowls flatter than most off-spinners and has been a tower of strength at county level in all types of cricket; in this picture he has just trapped Mike Smith of Warwickshire lbw in the Gillette Cup Final of 1972, which Lancashire won. Farokh Engineer joins in the appeal and umpire Charlie Elliott gives the decision

Below centre Fred Titmus, Middlesex and England, one of the greatest of Test off-spinners. His career spanned thirty-three years and he took 2,830 wickets, 153 of them in Test matches. Bill Alley glances at the action

Below right Pat Pocock, the Surrey off-spinner, who was recalled to the England side in 1984 at the age of thirty-seven after an absence of eight years. He took 7 wickets in 11 balls against Sussex in 1972

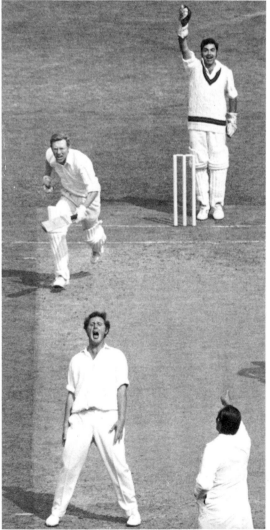

Bishen Bedi, one of the greatest slow left-arm spinners the world has seen. His skill lay equally in his variations of flight and in his control of spin. John Langridge is the umpire. Bedi took 1,560 wickets in his career, at an average of 21.69, and 266 Test wickets, and led India in twenty-two Test matches

Below left Dilip Doshi, who succeeded Bedi in the Indian Test team. A big spinner of the ball, he had a splendid season for Warwickshire in 1980 when he topped one hundred wickets

Below centre Bhagwat Chandrasekhar. One of the great mystery bowlers, Chandrasekhar was a leg-break bowler who concentrated mostly on the googly. In the 1970s he was one of the few bowlers capable of troubling Test sides on good wickets

Bhagwat Chandrasekhar
Career bowling: 1,063 wickets at 24.03
Test bowling: 242 wickets at 29.74

Below right Intikhab Alam, Surrey and Pakistan, the last of the international leg-break bowlers until the modern revival brought about by Qadir, Holland and Sivaramakrishnan. Intikhab took 125 wickets in his forty-seven Tests and he was also a hard-hitting batsman

Intikhab Alam
Career matches: 14,331 runs at 22.14, 1,571 wickets at 27.67
Test matches: 1,493 runs at 22.28, 125 wickets at 35.95

117

Beginning his career as Australia's wicket-keeper with the nickname 'Iron Gloves' for his seeming inability to take the ball cleanly, Rodney Marsh developed into a keeper second to none as a catcher of the ball. *Left* He flings himself to his right in spectacular fashion to take a one-handed catch offered by Tony Greig off the bowling of Gary Gilmour in the Prudential World Cup Semi-final at Headingley in 1975. Ian Chappell, the Australian captain, is at first slip. Gilmour took 6 for 14 in this match as England were bowled out for 93 on a damp wicket. *Below* Marsh's opposite number in his Tests against England was invariably Alan Knott. His anticipation and agility in keeping to his county and Test colleague Derek Underwood became renowned. Here he leaps to one side in balletic movement to catch Clive Lloyd one-handed off Underwood's bowling in the Lord's Test of 1976

Deryck Murray was probably the finest wicket-keeper to have represented the West Indies, adept at taking both pace and the spin of Lance Gibbs. He went to Nottingham and Cambridge universities and played for Warwickshire. Here he falls backwards as he catches Alan Hill of Derbyshire off the bowling of David Brown. Kanhai and A. C. Smith join the appeal

Wicket-keeper Catches

Undoubtedly, the two greatest wicket-keepers to have come out of the Indian sub-continent are Syed Kirmani of India and Wasim Bari of Pakistan.

Kirmani has kept to a variety of bowling, from the pace of Kapil Dev to the spin of Sivaramakrishnan and Venkataraghavan. He played a vital part in India's triumph in the Prudential World Cup of 1983, helping Kapil Dev in a match-winning stand against Zimbabwe at Tunbridge Wells and keeping brilliantly throughout the tournament

Right He dives to his left to hold a chance offered by David Gower off Mohinder Amarnath in the semi-final at Old Trafford – a desperately difficult catch in that Kirmani was able only to cling onto the ball between thumb and forefinger

Prudential World Cup, 1975. A magnificent sprawling catch by Wasim Bari off Naseer Malik to dismiss Rick McCosker of Australia. Mushtaq Mohammad joins in with an ecstatic appeal. Wasim Bari played a record eighty-one Test matches for Pakistan

119

Australians of the 1970s

The 1970s saw an Australian side of power in batting and bowling, which under the leadership of the Chappell brothers, was a formidable combination. *Left* Max Walker, a fast-medium bowler with a strange delivery and an ability to cut the ball away late, bowls to David Steele

Maxwell Henry Norman Walker

Career bowling: 135 matches, 499 wickets at 26.47
Test bowling: 34 matches, 138 wickets at 27.47

Below Left Jeff Thomson and his slinging action. Left arm outstretched, eyes focusing straight down the wicket, right arm and wrist cocked to deliver, Thomson became a fearsome opponent to all batsmen. This picture was taken at Melbourne, Australia, 1976. *Below right* Rick McCosker, seen in action during his century against England at Trent Bridge in 1977. He was a courageous opening batsman, successful captain of New South Wales and now a Test selector

Richard Bede McCosker

Career batting: 116 matches, 8,260 runs at 44.64
Test batting: 25 matches, 1,622 runs at 39.56

One of the most dependable of Australian batsmen was Ian Redpath of Victoria, which he represented from 1961 to 1976. Generally an opening batsman, Redpath is pictured right in action in his final, successful, series against the West Indies, 1975–6

Ian Ritchie Redpath
Career batting: 226 matches, 14,993 runs at
    41.99
Test batting: 66 matches, 4,737 runs at
    43.45

For the past fifteen years Australia has had a constant stream of fast bowlers. Below are three who span the generations: (*left*) an early picture of Dennis Lillee taken during the early part of the 1972 tour, his first to England. In 1984 he retired as a record breaker

Dennis Keith Lillee
Career bowling: 184 matches, 845 wickets
    at 22.86
Test bowling: 70 matches, 355 wickets at
    23.92

Centre Len Pascoe, son of Yugoslav immigrants, who for a brief time in the late seventies looked an even fiercer proposition than Dennis Lillee; (*right*) Rodney Hogg who shattered the Australian Test record with 41 wickets at 12.85 runs each in the 1978–9 series against Mike Brearley's England side. Hogg joined Lillee and Thomson in a formidable array of fast bowlers when that pair returned from World Series Cricket.

There was never a moment in the 1970s and early 1980s when opposing batsmen could gain refuge from the ferocity of the Australian attack.

Boycott's Hundredth Hundred

Few cricketers have excited as much publicity or conflicting reaction as Geoffrey Boycott. He is the only cricketer to have twice averaged more than 100 in an English first-class season and his aggregate of 8,114 runs in 108 Test matches is a world record. It is a record that could have been even better had he not been banned from Test cricket for his involvement in the South African venture in 1981–2 and had he not chosen to exile himself from Test cricket, for reasons never clearly explained, between 1974 and 1977 during which time he missed thirty Tests.

It was not surprising that when Boycott announced he was again available for selection for the England side in 1977 he should be surrounded with much publicity and with BBC television cameras and reporters monitoring every moment of his return.

It was a most appropriate season for Boycott to reappear in the Test arena, for he began the year with Yorkshire on ninety-three centuries. He hit four hundreds in June and July which ensured that he would be recalled to the England side at Trent Bridge, where he scored his ninety-eighth century in England's victory. His ninety-ninth was scored against Warwickshire on the Saturday, and he went on to Leeds for his hundredth.

The fourth Test match at Headingley was a double triumph. England won by an innings and regained the Ashes, and Boycott hit 191 so becoming the first batsman ever to score his hundredth hundred in a Test match.

Above The classic drive through the off-side during his century at Trent Bridge. Rodney Marsh, an old adversary, is the wicket-keeper. *Below* In the match that followed, Boycott led Yorkshire against Warwickshire at Edgbaston. In spite of rain, he hit 104, his ninety-ninth century. Geoff Humpage is the wicket-keeper as Boycott considers a run to leg

Above Geoff Boycott on-drives a ball from Greg Chappell for the fourteenth boundary of his innings and reaches a hundred hundreds off the 232nd ball of his innings. Hookes and McCosker are the patient slips

Left Boycott lifts his arms in triumph as he acknowledges the roar of his home crowd, ecstatic at the fairy-tale conclusion of events

Below Boycott has lost his cap in the celebrations that followed his four off Chappell. It was later returned to him by the supporter who took it. Roope chats to him while Barry Henson, the *Daily Express* photographer based in Leeds, gets closer for a picture in spite of police presence

Below Boycott, having mopped himself down with the towel he is holding, watches the television replay of the stroke that brought him his hundredth hundred. He holds a glass of champagne while Peter West asks him for comment and shares the enjoyment

Above The triumphant return by Boycott culminated in his hundredth hundred, in a Test match, on his own ground. At the end he is hurried from the field by a BBC technician. The hurry is because the BBC is anxious to interview Boycott before transmission ends for the day

Below Peter West has now been given the towel as he interviews Boycott on the Headingley dressing-room balcony. The camera is focused on the man-of-the-moment who still holds his glass of champagne

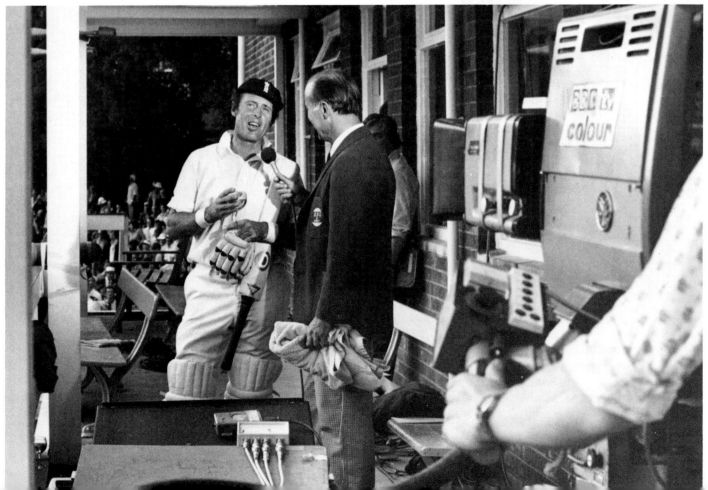

Right Encouraged by the television technician, Boycott lifts his glass of champagne and acknowledges the crowd. A deeply sensitive man for whom an abundance of success has caused intense personal problems, Boycott has not always found it easy to maintain a sympathetic relationship with the public or media. Sometimes he has seen enemies and criticism where none has existed; at other times he has seen battles to be dourly fought when others saw joy rather than attrition. On Thursday, 11 August 1977, however, the prodigal son had returned to the fold and he saluted his fellow Yorkshiremen to whom, in his own way, he has always remained deeply committed

Left The Yorkshire crowd acclaim their hero. Boycott is on the balcony and has just been urged to raise his glass as a toast to his followers. They respond with enthusiasm and joy. The England banners are outnumbered by those which celebrate their man

Right Yorkshire has produced three of the greatest opening batsmen in the history of the game, Geoffrey Boycott, Herbert Sutcliffe and Sir Leonard Hutton. On Saturday, 13 August 1977, at the instigation of Yorkshire secretary Joe Lister, the three were pictured together at Headingley. As a Yorkshireman in exile, Ken Kelly was given the honour of helping to organise the picture which found a place in *Wisden*. Boycott, having completed his hundredth hundred, wears his England sweater and kneels beside the wheelchair in which sits Herbert Sutcliffe who hit 150 centuries in the years between the two world wars. On the right kneels Len Hutton who, in spite of losing the war years, hit 129 centuries and became one of England's most renowned captains

Three Outstanding Fast Bowlers

Three pace men of contrasting styles who did much to lift their sides.

Left John Lever, fast-medium left-arm bowler with an easy, rhythmical action. After 103 years without success, Essex entered a period in 1979 when triumph followed triumph: three County Championships, two John Player League titles and the Benson and Hedges Cup in the space of six seasons. The key to those triumphs was the bowling of John Lever who took 100 wickets in a season in 1978, 1979, 1983 and 1984. Twice he was named as Players' Player of the Year and his unquenchable enthusiasm and endeavour have made him one of the most popular men in the game. 'An international bowler by any standard', he has taken 67 wickets in twenty Tests

Below left Keith Boyce, the West Indian whose all-round cricket delighted followers of Essex in the 1970s. He had a short, successful Test career, the high point being the 1973 series against England, when he took 19 wickets averaging 15.47 in the three matches, and also averaged 25.80 with the bat; but it was his performances as fast bowler and fierce hitter that won the hearts of the crowd at county level. Injury ended his career prematurely and robbed him of the opportunity of sharing in Essex's years of glory
Below right Richard Collinge, the New Zealand fast left-arm bowler who took 116 Test wickets, a record at the time of his retirement in 1978

Keith David Boyce
Career matches: 285 matches, 8,800 runs at 23.29, 852 wickets at 25.02
Test matches: 21 matches, 657 runs at 24.33, 60 wickets at 30.01

Richard Owen Collinge
Career bowling: 163 matches, 524 wickets at 24.41
Test bowling: 35 matches, 116 wickets at 29.25

Botham caught Dujon bowled Marshall, The Oval, 1984

Lamb lbw bowled Marshall, The Oval, 1984. Dujon, in particular, celebrates!

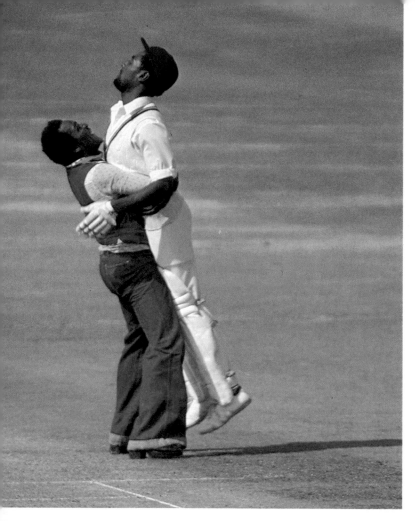

Left Vivian Richards receives a big celebration hug after his century at Trent Bridge in 1976. He went on to score 232

Above John Lever removes a dog from the pitch at The Oval, 1977, much to the amusement of Bob Woolmer

Below The Trent Bridge Jester, Derek Randall, carries off the lady physiotherapist at Trent Bridge, 1977. She was employed by the Club and by the TCCB for that Test Match

The Chappell Brothers

Grandsons of Victor Richardson who captained South Australia for many years and also captained Australia in South Africa in 1935/36 and was vice-captain of the 1930 Australian touring side to England, the Chappell brothers dominated Australian cricket for two decades. Ian Chappell (*below left*) was born in 1943 and played the first of his seventy-five Test matches for Australia in December 1964. He took over as Australia's captain from Bill Lawry in 1971, and in the next few years transformed the side into a ruthlessly efficient organisation, capitalising on the fiery bowling of Lillee and Thomson, his own and his brother Greg's batting, and the aggressive wicket-keeping of Rodney Marsh. Ian Chappell's side was broken up by World Series Cricket, in which he was a leading protagonist, but by that time he had handed over the captaincy to his younger brother Greg (*right*) who was born in 1948.

A tall and elegant cricketer, Greg Chappell batted with dignity and grace although his captaincy was as hard as his brother's. Greg made his Test debut in December 1970, when he scored 108 against England at Perth. He was to play in eighty-seven Tests, hit twenty-four centuries and score 7,110 Test runs, surpassing Don Bradman's record in his final Test against Pakistan in Sydney in January 1984. There was a calm authority in Greg Chappell's cricket which was sharpened by an acute knowledge of the game. He spent one season with Somerset and he complemented his batting with brilliant fielding at slip and medium-pace bowling of quality enough to take nearly fifty Test wickets.

The youngest of the three brothers, Trevor (*below right*), has met with less success than Ian and Greg, but like his brothers he has played for Australia, as a tenacious batsman and useful medium-pace bowler. He was noted in Packer's World Series Cricket and scored freely for New South Wales so that he earned a place on the 1981 tour to England, but he played in only three Tests with limited success. His qualities are better suited to the one-day game, and he was in the Australian squad for the 1983 Prudential World Cup.

Contrasting English Captains

Mike Brearley is accepted as one of the greatest captains of the modern era and his record justifies the acclaim that he has been given. He led Middlesex from 1971 to 1982 and they won the Championship four times under his leadership. An academic of distinction, he allied his tactical awareness and probing insight of the game to a concern for and understanding of the men under him. Relentless in pursuing the weaknesses of opponents, he managed all in a relaxed and friendly manner. *Left* He is being interviewed by Steve Lee of BBC Midlands as he pads up for the last Championship game of 1982. Middlesex's success in this match at Worcester assured them of the title and Brearley retired from the game although he did make one appearance the following season. Few men could have been so relaxed or welcomed an interviewer at such a time.

As a batsman he was perhaps not quite up to Test standard, but as a slip fielder he had few equals. Early in his career he had been a wicket-keeper. *Below* He falls to his left to take a juggling catch to dismiss New Zealand captain Mark Burgess off the bowling of Phil Edmonds. The Test was at Trent Bridge and Brearley led England to victory in this series in 1978. Taylor is the wicket-keeper

Brearley came into prominence as vice-captain to Tony Greig in 1976–7 and took over from Greig when the tall all-rounder defected to World Series Cricket. The two men were different in character.

John Michael Brearley
Career batting: 455 matches, 25,185 runs at 37.81
Test batting: 39 matches, 1,442 runs at 22.88

Tony Greig, seen right in typically aggressive mood against the Australians, was a dashing and controversial cricketer who was in a hurry to succeed. He was born in South Africa of Scottish parents and moved to Sussex in 1966. Essentially a front-footed attacking batsman, he bowled medium pace and could swing the ball appreciably. On occasions, as at Port of Spain in 1974 when he took a match-winning 13 wickets, he bowled off-breaks.

At Test level he was an inspiring, if impetuous, captain, and he led England from the doldrums that they had suffered in the early seventies. Yet his attitude to the game aroused mixed reactions. He became notorious for running out Kallicharran after the final ball of the day had been bowled, an action for which he apologised; the West Indian batsman was reinstated. He attempted to match the Australian aggression with an aggression of his own which many felt violated the spirit of the game. In the picture below, taken during the Old Trafford Test in 1977, the Australian fielders, Marsh in particular, turn in horror as Greig defiantly stands his ground after having, as the Australians claimed and television cameras confirmed, touched a ball from Thomson to the wicket-keeper. Greig adopted a policy of not walking which he believed followed the Australian line and on this occasion he got away with it. Tony Greig now lives in Australia, and he is one of the principal cricket commentators on Channel 9.

Anthony William Greig
Career matches: 350 matches, 16,660 runs at 31.19, 856 wickets at 28.85
Test matches: 58 matches, 3,599 runs at 40.43, 141 wickets at 32.20

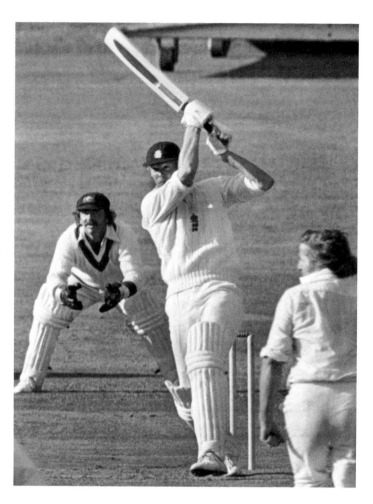

Rain Stopped Play
The dismal sight of Lord's during the Centenary Test in 1980. What should have been a celebratory and festive occasion is ruined by the weather. The covers are firmly in position and the ground staff move about mournfully reviewing the situation on a ground bereft of spectators

Misery for the cricket-lover can be joy for others. A groundsman looks on at Edgbaston in 1968 as two mallard ducks from the nearby Cannon Hill Park relish the puddles that have formed on the outfield

The ground staff at Edgbaston in 1969 work forlornly in desolate conditions. It was a struggle to make play possible, but the fight was a vain one. The power of the elements proved too strong

Above left The ground staff at Worcester use an old mangle to wring out the cloths used for drying up the pitch in an effort to get the Gillette Cup semi-final between Worcestershire and Lancashire under way, August 1974. Although an old-fashioned method, it worked perfectly, and clubs such as Worcestershire have to work within a strict financial budget

Above right Alan Smith and Lance Gibbs take cover at Edgbaston and their faces reveal little hope of play
Below The hope of the future. The new motorised covers at Edgbaston which protect the whole surface of the ground and leave it ready for immediate play as soon as the rain stops

Stumped! Run Out!
Alan Knott stumps Farokh Engineer, the Lancashire wicket-keeper, in the Gillette Cup Final of 1974. The ball, bowled by James Graham-Brown, spun wide off Engineer's boot, but Knott took it cleanly and pulled off a brilliant stumping. He was later named as Man-of-the-Match

Right Mike Gatting is lucky to get a not out verdict as Geoff Humpage whips off the bails with Gatting's toe off the ground in a Warwickshire–Middlesex John Player League game in 1980

Kallicharran is left stranded by a turning ball from Vic Marks and Derek Taylor, a fine county keeper, stumps him with ease

Bob Taylor breaks the wicket and Gavaskar is run out by yards after Randall's pick up and throw from mid-wicket, England v India, Edgbaston, 1979. Randall is on the left of the picture

Right Bowler Ian Botham goes down the wicket and throws to run out Richard Hadlee who has attempted to take a quick single off his bowling, England v New Zealand, Lord's, 1978

A brilliant piece of fielding by Mike Gatting runs out Javed Miandad, England v Pakistan, Edgbaston, 1982. Gatting flicked the ball at the stumps from short-leg as Javed had edged forward. It was a moment of lightning reflex on the part of Gatting, and photographer Ken Kelly

Physical Fitness

Under the guidance of Bernard Thomas, the fitness of the England quick bowlers is checked before an overseas tour. The tests are thorough and take a day at Thomas's Health Clinic and in the nets at Edgbaston County Cricket Ground.

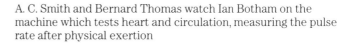

A. C. Smith and Bernard Thomas watch Ian Botham on the machine which tests heart and circulation, measuring the pulse rate after physical exertion

Below left Chris Old bowling in the nets under the watchful eye of Alec Bedser. Willis, Dilley and Miller are also engaged

Below Ian Botham blows into a machine that measures vital capacity, ie the speed of the air coming out of the lungs, and for how long the exhalation can be sustained

Peter Willey, watched by gymnasium assistant Jimmy Dunn, the former West Bromwich Albion footballer, works on the jogging machine. His right knee is heavily strapped, but he still passes the fitness test

Below Ian Botham on the Dynavit machine. The clip attached to the left ear measures the pulse rate in the midst of strenuous physical exertion. Alan Smith and Ken Barrington look on in amusement. This was shortly before the side left for West Indies in 1980–1. Ken Barrington, the assistant manager, died of a heart attack on that tour

Below right Dilley takes his turn in the nets. Miller, Old and Willis await their turn

Hat Tricks

At Edgbaston, at the beginning of July 1974, England beat India by an innings and 78 runs. Striving to save the game, India were 59 for 4 in their second innings when Naik was joined by Ashok Mankad. In a stubborn stand of 87 the pair gave India hope of survival until Mankad, in keeping down a short-pitched delivery from Chris Old, jerked off his cap. *Left* Greig watches from slip as the cap falls. *Below* Fletcher and Knott walk forwards trying to conceal their delight as Mankad, in justified disgust, gazes at the wicket which his falling cap has broken. It was the third incident in a Test match since World War II in which a batsman was out hit wicket because his cap dislodged a bail.

Allan Lamb and Chris Old are luckier than Mankad. *Far right* Old himself comes perilously close to suffering Mankad's fate a year later when, troubled by the fearsome Lillee, he loses his cap but not his wicket. *Right* Seven years on and the helmet has replaced the cap, but the outcome is nearly the same. Allan Lamb loses his helmet in ducking under an Imran bouncer. Perplexed by the presence of helmet and ball, he is lucky to escape dismissal by one or the other.

Opposite below Running true to form, Mike Smith scurries for the crease with Jim Cumbes keeping pace, neck and neck. Younis Ahmed looks on as Cumbes takes aim and misses the stumps from two yards. All that Mike Smith loses is his cap which floats back defiantly towards Cumbes. Warwickshire *v* Surrey, John Player League, July 1969

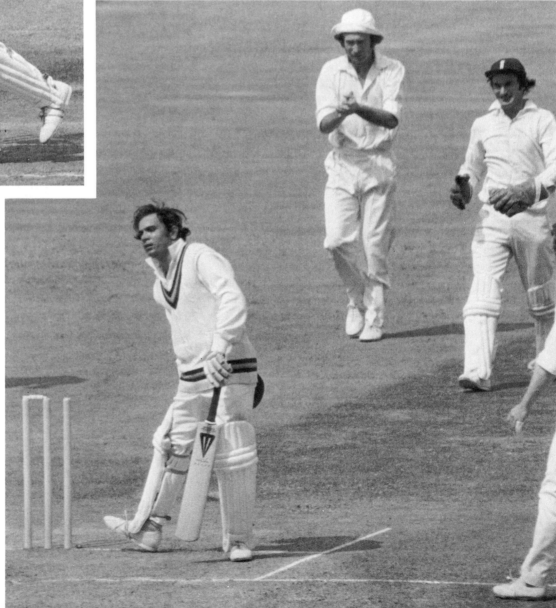

Batsmen

Imran Khan hits out lustily, taking a six off the bowling of Eddie Hemmings, during his innings of 65 at Edgbaston. Bob Taylor is the wicket-keeper. England v Pakistan, 1982.

One of the world's top all-rounders, Imran developed into a great fast bowler, but when injury prevented him from bowling for more than a year, he could still hold his place in a Test side as a batsman. His bowling has gone through many phases, from medium pace in-swingers to really fast, but his batting has been more consistent.

He is a naturally attacking player. He gave substance and panache to Sussex, and inspired Pakistan, as a player and as a captain, to their finest performances in international cricket.

Below left Gordon Greenidge came to England as a child, and could have qualified to play for England. He first played for Hampshire in 1970, and made his debut for Barbados three years later.

Greenidge is one of the most exciting opening batsmen that Test cricket has ever known. He has scored close to 27,000 runs in first-class cricket and, as well as starring for the West Indies in more than seventy Tests, he has excited English crowds with his batting for Hampshire. At one time he held the individual record in all the limited-over competitions.

He is seen here hooking the ball for 4 off his eyebrows. This shot brought him his 200 at Lord's in 1984.

Below Brian Close, a left-handed batsman, a right-arm bowler of both seam and spin, and a captain of great courage. He was the youngest player to achieve the 'double', at the age of eighteen in 1949. In this picture he is facing the West Indies at Trent Bridge in 1976, when he was recalled to the England side. Deryck Murray is the wicket-keeper and Alvin Kallicharran is at slip.

Close was renowned for his toughness and determination, both as a leader of men and as a close fielder. He captained Yorkshire and England, was sacked by both and then inspired the revival of Somerset cricket.

He was also a good soccer player, appearing for Leeds United, Arsenal and Bradford City.

Dennis Brian Close

Career matches: 783 matches, 34,911 runs at 33.24, 1,168 wickets at 26.40
Test matches: 22 matches, 887 runs at 25.34, 18 wickets at 29.55

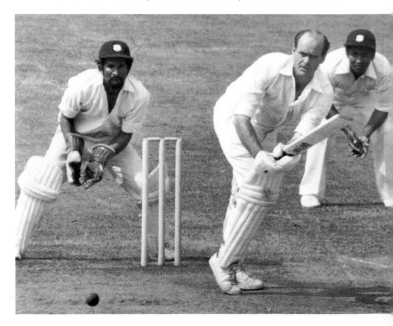

Majid Khan is the son of Dr Mohammad Jahangir Khan, who played for Cambridge University and India, and the cousin of Imran Khan and Javed Burki, both of Pakistan.

He was a brilliant stroke maker, a fine attacking opening or middle-order batsman, who was not afraid of hitting the ball 'over the top'.

Majid was a richly gifted all-round cricketer, whose sixty-three Test appearances constituted a record for Pakistan at one time.

He served Glamorgan well, and was the most popular of cricketers, accepted as such in all cricketing countries.

Majid scored seventy-three first-class centuries, with a highest score of 241.

Majid Jahangir Khan
Career batting: 407 matches, 27,328 runs at 42.90
Test batting: 63 matches, 3,931 runs at 38.92

Below right Desmond Haynes relaxes on his bat during the Test match against England at Trent Bridge in 1980. A splendid batsman, calm and enterprising, Haynes first played for Barbados in 1977, and opened for the West Indies a year later. He and Gordon Greenidge established the most formidable opening partnership in world cricket, one that should continue for a number of years.

Haynes is a fine fielder, in any position; of late he has fielded close to the wicket, being a good short-leg to the bowling of Roger Harper.

One of his finest innings was his 184 in 490 minutes at Lord's during the 1980 tour.

Below Bev Congdon was another captain with fine leadership qualities. Like all good generals, he led from the front, and was also one of New Zealand's finest batsmen.

In 1973, captaining his country against England, he scored 176 at Trent Bridge and 175 in the following Test at Lord's. He brought his side to the brink of victory in both cases. The picture reproduced shows him in action during the Lord's Test. Although victories in England were denied him, he led New Zealand to their first victory over Australia, and was in the side that beat England at Wellington, for the first time ever, in 1978. A fitting climax for a fine cricketer who, in a career that spanned eighteen years, saw a great change in the fortunes of New Zealand cricket.

Bevan Ernest Congdon
Career matches: 241 matches, 13,101 runs at 34.84, 204 wickets at 30.02
Test matches: 61 matches, 3,448 runs at 32.22, 59 wickets at 36.50

141

Lillee Wickets

In 1981 Dennis Lillee toured England for the last time. He took 39 wickets at an average of 22.30 in this six-match series of Tests.

Lillee claims the wicket of Peter Willey lbw. As Willey walks to the pavilion, Australian captain Kim Hughes congratulates the bowler. Lillee took 8 wickets for 80 runs in this first Test at Trent Bridge

Centre At Headingley in the third Test Lillee took 7 wickets for 143 runs. In this important wicket Ian Botham is caught by Rodney Marsh to give him his 264th wicket-keeping victim in Test matches, thus beating Alan Knott's world record. As Knott played again for England later and took his total to 269, Marsh went ahead and overtook him once again. Marsh retired with 355 Test match victims behind the wicket, taken in ninety-six Test matches for Australia

Below right Another wicket for Lillee at Headingley. Graham Gooch is well caught by Terry Alderman fielding at third slip, who dived to his left in front of Border at second slip. As a bowler, Alderman claimed 42 wickets in this series at an average of 21.26 runs each

The Catch of the Day

Opposite England *v* Australia, Prudential Trophy, Edgbaston, June 1981. With England chasing a target of 250, a reluctant streaker provides a diversion. No doubt influenced by the first five letters of the sponsor's name, he covers his manliness, with an unsmiling Marsh in pursuit.

In the second picture Marsh, who had missed two straightforward chances behind the stumps, makes his first catch of the day. Gatting, on his way to a valiant 96, is amused. Rodney Marsh then completes the catch, both hands cupping the chance safely. As Richie Benaud said in a BBC broadcast, 'The only thing he's caught all day'.

The arms of the law take over from Marsh and the intruder, his day's cricket nearing its close, is marched past Graeme Wood.

The final picture shows the streaker leaving the arena to an amused ovation from spectators. In keeping with decorum, the policewoman brings up the rear.

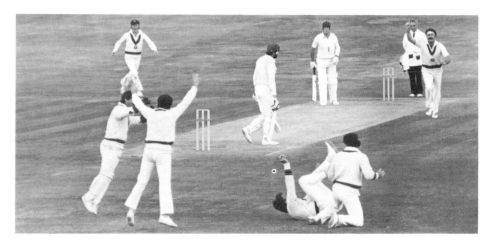

Australians, 1981

The 1981 Ashes series in England saw England, inspired by the performances of Ian Botham and Bob Willis, come from behind to win a remarkable rubber. While most of the plaudits went to Botham, Australia had her own heroes, not least of whom was Allan Border who, batting with a broken finger, hit 123 not out at Old Trafford in a brave attempt to stave off defeat and save the Ashes. He is seen in action (*left*). Mike Whitney is the other batsman.

Above He receives a pain-killing spray. *Below* He leaves the field to the applause of the England side, but Australia are beaten

In the final Test match at The Oval, Australia introduced Dirk Wellham. *Top right* Wellham takes off his cap in relief and joy on having reached his century on his Test debut. He had been on 99 for 25 minutes. *Centre* He slips and sits down in avoiding a Botham bouncer while he is on 99. *Below* Botham turns away unsmiling and Wellham ponders if the hundredth run will ever come. Wellham became the first Australian since H. Graham in 1893 to score 100 in England on his Test debut.

A Moment of History

Glenn Turner turns a ball from Gladstone Small to leg during his innings of 311 not out for Worcestershire against Warwickshire, 29 May 1982. This was Turner's hundredth hundred and it was a salutary reminder to Warwickshire that they had rejected him when he came to England from New Zealand recommended by 'Billy' Ibadulla, and intent on making a career in cricket. He scored 2,636 first-class runs and eleven centuries against Warwickshire.

When Turner completed his hundredth hundred his mentor, 'Billy' Ibadulla, the former Warwickshire player, walked out to the wicket with a celebratory gin and tonic. In the first picture, Ibadulla shakes hands with his pupil; then he pours out the gin and tonic while Dennis Amiss looks on; finally Turner drinks while wicket-keeper Geoff Humpage offers his congratulations. It should be noted that Willis bowled only twelve overs during the Worcestershire innings

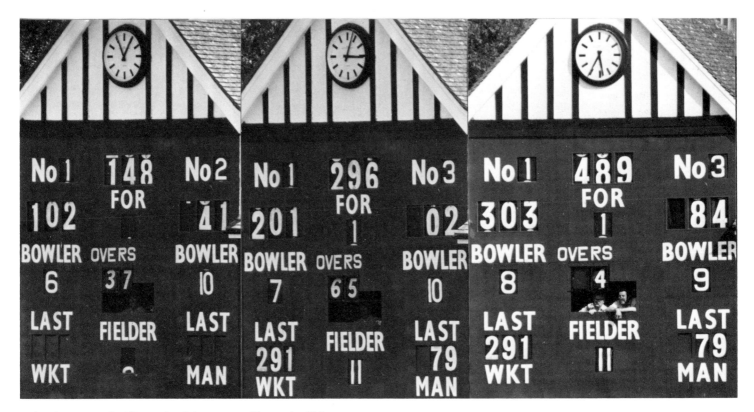

A unique record of Turner's triple century. He reached his hundredth hundred at 12.55pm, having batted for 115 minutes before lunch, out of a total of 148 runs scored. At 3.03pm the double century is reached out of 296 in sixty-five overs. The third picture shows Turner on 303 out of 489 at 5.38pm. Dipak Patel is the number 3 batsman. Ken Kelly had sensed that this would be the setting for Turner's hundredth hundred and had set himself up accordingly

Right Turner stands in front of the scoreboard at the end of his innings

Ibadulla and Turner clink glasses as Worcestershire Cathedral provides the background to the historic occasion

Changing Attitudes

Over the past twenty years cricket players have become more demonstrative in expressing their congratulations on their team-mates' achievements.

The top picture records a historic event. Only thirty-one bowlers in the history of the game have taken 2,000 wickets in a career and Eric Hollies, the Warwickshire leg-spinner, reached that milestone on 28 June 1955, bowling George Dews to reach his 2,000. Dews walks away and Jack Bannister shakes hands with Hollies while the others turn and *walk* towards the veteran bowler. Hollies had been playing first-class cricket since 1932. Although he was to take 115 wickets in the season, his career of thirteen Tests was already five years in the past.

The bottom picture shows the ritual dance by the West Indian fielders after Milton Small had had David Gower caught at slip by Clive Lloyd. It was Small's third wicket in two Test matches – he was to take another later in the innings – and his thirty-second wicket in his tenth first-class match. It is 30 June 1984, and Viv Richards begins the celebrations as Gower walks away. Six players are already slapping hands with Small. One wonders what they would have done for Eric Hollies!

Bob Willis

In 1975, Bob Willis was threatened with an abrupt end to his career. Operations on both knees left them badly scarred and the future in doubt. He was determined to play cricket again and under the guidance of Bernard Thomas he set out on a vigorous programme that hopefully would restore him to full fitness.

Right The road back was long and arduous. Hours were spent in the gymnasium engaged in exercises aimed at building up body weight, strength and stamina so that once again Bob Willis would be able to bowl at 90mph

Below He begins his training on the cycle in the gymnasium; the scars are clearly visible, but so too is the encouragement given by Bernard Thomas

Below right Through sheer dedication, and a determination not to be beaten, Bob Willis is back in action and the most hostile English bowler of his generation is once more pounding in with fire in his eyes and in his heart

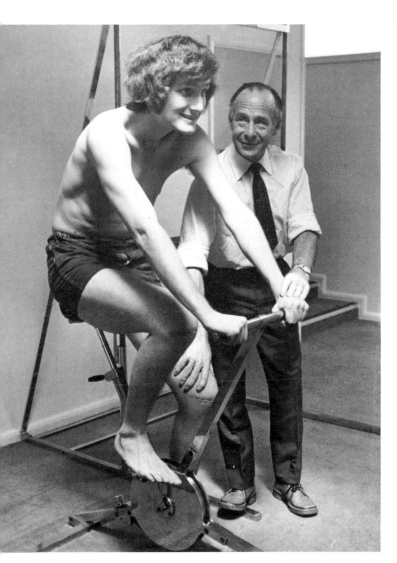

Restored to full fitness, Bob Willis played a vital part in England's historic winning of the Ashes series in 1981. In the fifth Test match at Old Trafford in August, he achieved the all-important breakthrough on the last day which led to an England victory.
Right Ray Bright falls to a spectacular tumbling catch by Alan Knott. Mike Brearley, the England skipper, supports the appeal energetically

Middle right In 1982, Bob Willis became captain of England. A leader by inspiration rather than by tactical genius, he shares the taste of success with England team-mates Jackman, Marks, Fowler and Botham, sipping champagne as he holds the Cornhill Trophy after the victory over Pakistan at Headingley

Bottom right The captaincy of England represented a splendid reward for the relentless efforts that Willis had made to regain fitness. He enjoyed the position, and here shares a joke with Her Majesty the Queen as he introduces the England players to her at Lord's in 1982

Below The pinnacle of achievement. Allan Lamb dives forward to accept a bat-pad catch off Martin Crowe to give Bob Willis his 299th wicket in Test cricket. England *v* New Zealand, Headingley, 1983. Later in the day, with New Zealand pressing for the first-ever victory over England in England, Bob Willis knocks Jeff Crowe's middle stump out of the ground. It is his 300th Test wicket, and only one other Englishman, Freddie Trueman, has reached the mark before him

In 1984, Bob Willis was forced to return home from Pakistan unwell, and David Gower took over the England captaincy. Gower was retained as England captain for the series against the West Indies, but Willis was also retained for his bowling for the first three Test matches of the series.

The third Test was played at Headingley, the scene of Willis' greatest triumphs. He had an early success when Greenidge was caught by Botham off his bowling, but thereafter he was the victim of a violent assault on the England attack by Michael Holding. Willis conceded 123 in eighteen overs. *Above* Holding eventually skies the ball to Allott. Willis watches in apprehension. Two catches have already been dropped off his bowling as Holding has hit him mercilessly. Allott makes the catch and Paul Downton applauds. For Willis, hands on hips, there is no elation, simply relief and resignation. It is his 325th, and last, Test wicket. A glorious career is at an end

Fast bowling is a tiring business. Willis relaxes and contemplates on a career that brought him 880 wickets and saw him bowl for fifteen years, the last fourteen of them for England

The ICC Trophy

In 1979 and 1982, as preludes to the Prudential World Cup, the ICC held a competition for associate members, the winners qualifying for a place in the world cup tournament itself. Sri Lanka were winners of the first tournament, but by 1982 they had attained Test status and the final was fought between Zimbabwe and Bermuda. Zimbabwe won the Trophy and went on to acquit themselves splendidly in the 1983 Prudential World Cup, beating Australia and running India very close in a memorable match at Tunbridge Wells.

The ICC Trophy matches were played on picturesque club grounds in the Midlands, like Kings Heath, Birmingham, but unfortunately the tournament was badly hit by the weather. This did not stop Bermuda and Bangladesh who played under lowering cloud in the game at Kings Heath (*left*). The friendly spirit in which the tournament was fought is captured in the attacking style of Vavine Pala of Papua New Guinea (*below left*) who excelled in hitting sixes and enjoying English beer – a batsman in the Colin Milburn mould. One of the stars of the tournament was Kevin Curran, the Zimbabwe all-rounder (*below*) who, in the World Cup itself, played an innings of 62 against the West Indies. Jeff Dujon is the wicket-keeper. Curran is now with Gloucestershire.

Zimbabwe were the strongest side in the competition in 1982 and Duncan Fletcher (*right*) receives the Trophy from Gubby Allen. Fletcher (*below centre*) is one of the finest cricketers that Zimbabwe have produced, an excellent all-rounder who won the Man-of-the-Match award in the victory over Australia at Trent Bridge in 1983 when he scored 69 not out and took 4 for 42. He is now in South Africa and his experience is being used by Western Province. Zimbabwe are particularly strong in all-rounders and Peter Rawson (*below left*) was particularly effective as a bowler throughout the competition, his brisk medium pace troubling most batsmen. The most experienced of the Zimbabwe players is John Traicos (*below right*), who played three Test matches for South Africa in 1970 and is an off-break bowler. He was born in Egypt of Greek parents. Traicos was vice-captain to Fletcher and led Zimbabwe when the all-rounder stepped down, but, at the age of thirty-eight, Traicos relinquished the captaincy in 1985 although he continued to represent his country.

Moments of Triumph

In 1983, the third Prudential World Cup resulted in an unexpected triumph for India who beat the West Indies in the Final at Lord's.

In the semi-final at Old Trafford they had a six-wicket win over England. 'Man-of-the-Match' Mohindar Amarnath was the architect of victory. His gentle medium-pace bowling gave him 2 wickets for 27 runs in twelve overs. His innings of 46, in a 92-run third wicket partnership with Yashpal Sharma, set the scene for India to coast home with a comfortable margin of thirty-two balls to spare.

The final at Lord's was a great triumph for India. Their opponents, the West Indies, were the clear favourites to win the cup for the third time, but India won with unexpected ease in an exciting low-scoring final.

The Man-of-the-Match was again Mohindar Amarnath who, with bowling figures of 3 wickets for 12 runs in seven overs, and an innings of 26 runs, gave the major contribution to this Indian victory. All the other bowlers played their part and bowled magnificently to restrict the West Indies to a total of 140.

Of the batsmen, Srikkanth with 38, the top scorer of the match, Patil with 27, and later, batsman Madan Lal and Kirmani with 17 and 14 respectively, played valuable roles in the Indian victory by 43 runs, and won a place in cricketing history.

Madan Lal opens a bottle of champagne against the wind, but does not seem to mind the resultant spray as India celebrate their semi-final victory over England at Old Trafford
Left Mohinder Amarnath square cuts for four in the Final. Amarnath played a responsible innings and bowled economically, and he was named Man-of-the-Match
Below left The highest innings of the Final came from Srikkanth, the Indian opening batsman. He played some scintillating shots in his innings of 38 and here he slashes a boundary
Below Kapil Dev, the Indian captain, ends the England innings in the semi-final when he bowls opposing captain Bob Willis. Kapil Dev took 3 for 35 in his eleven overs

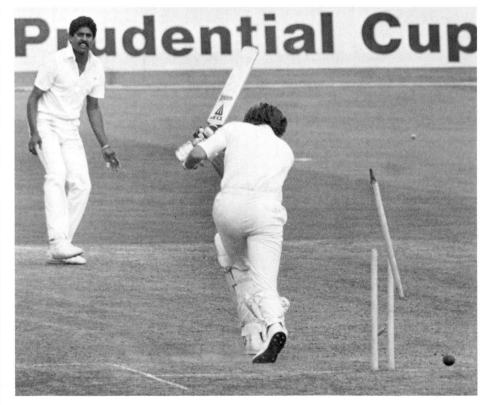

Historic Win

New Zealand first toured England in 1931, and in 1983, at Headingley, after seventeen defeats and eleven draws, they notched their first victory in a Test match in England.

They bowled England out for 225 in their first innings, with only four England players making double figures. Chris Tavaré with 69, Allan Lamb 58, Ian Botham 38 and wicket-keeper Bob Taylor scored 10. For New Zealand, Lance Cairns took 7 wickets for 74, and Jeremy Coney 2 wickets for 21.

In the New Zealand first innings total of 377, John Wright scored 93 and Bruce Edgar hit 84, with Richard Hadlee chipping in with 75. So they had a lead of 152 runs. England only totalled 252 in their second innings, with David Gower scoring 112 not out. He eventually ran out of partners with only Allan Lamb making runs. He was the next highest scorer with 28. The New Zealand bowlers had paved the way to victory, Ewen Chatfield taking 5 wickets for 95 and Lance Cairns 3 wickets for 70. Cairns, with match figures of 10 wickets for 144, was given the Man-of-the-Match award.

With New Zealand having to score only 101 for victory, they lost 5 wickets before the historic win was achieved.

The man who scored the winning run, Jeremy Coney, was quoted as saying: 'The main feeling was thinking of all the New Zealand players who have been coming here for fifty-two years, better players than myself, and making sure that their sweat and effort had not been in vain.' Historic words indeed, and a fitting tribute to all those players.

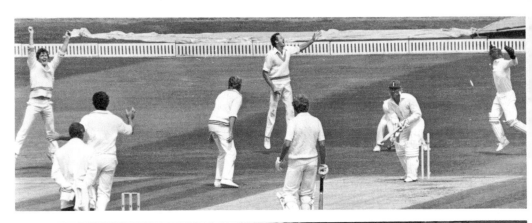

Two of Cairns' wickets are shown in the pictures (*above*). In England's second innings, Bob Taylor (*top*) is bowled by Cairns for 9. John Wright, Jeremy Coney and wicket-keeper Ian Smith jump for joy. In the second picture Martin Crowe, helmeted, turns away and tosses the ball in the air in delight, having just caught Norman Cowans for 10 off Cairns' bowling to end the England innings

Skipper Geoff Howarth pops the champagne cork and a victorious and happy team pose for their moment of glory (*below*). Names of players, back row left to right: John Bracewell, Martin Crowe, Ewen Chatfield, Jeff Crowe, Ian Smith, Trevor Franklin; front row left to right: Sir Alan Wright (manager), John Wright, Geoff Howorth, Lance Cairns, Richard Hadlee, Jeremy Coney, Bruce Edgar, Martin Snedden

The Art of Fast Bowling
Left Imran Khan, one of the great fast bowlers of Test cricket. He is a disciple of the fitness cult and has worked hard to develop his strength in the upper body. The power in arm and shoulder is seen at the point of delivery, and the aggression is reflected in the follow-through

Right Michael Holding, one of the very greatest fast bowlers of the modern era. There is a silky smoothness in his run to the wicket and a magnificent leap into the delivery stride so that the whole action is one of latent power and unmistakeable beauty

Bob Willis was a fast bowler from the heart rather than from inherent technique. His 325 Test wickets are a testimony to the speed, hostility and determination of the man who overcame serious injury to continue to bowl fast for England

Below Dennis Lillee displaying one of the outstanding fast bowling actions of any age. With umpire Bill Alley looking on, Lillee is seen at the beginning and end of his delivery stride. He comes in straight, close to the stumps, and lands on his right foot for the perfect follow-through

Above Richard Hadlee, the greatest fast bowler in New Zealand's cricket history and an outstanding all-rounder. He has the most economic action in modern cricket and the correctness of the action, as demonstrated in the photographs, allows him to bowl his lethal outswinger

Mike Procter, the great South African all-rounder who was a tower of strength for Gloucestershire and who bowled very, very quickly. His was not the perfect action. His arm action is in advance of his body action and his full weight comes through with the body at the end

Neil Foster, England's new fast bowling hope. He took 11 for 163 in the Test at Madras, 1984–5, and virtually won England the match, and the series

Fast Bowling

A view of the pressure put on batsmen by fast bowlers. Dennis Lillee is bowling to Geoff Boycott with eight men clustered round the bat. Boycott gets on his toes to smother the lifting ball

Geoff Lawson, who has succeeded Dennis Lillee as the spearhead of Australia's attack. He leaps high into the delivery stride, his left leg points towards the batsman, and he follows through strongly. Donald Oslear is the umpire

Gladstone Small has all ten fielders in the picture as he bowls for Warwickshire against Surrey at Edgbaston in 1984. The appeal for lbw on Feltham is rejected, but the pressure from fast bowler and captain Gifford is maintained. Warwickshire, however, did not win the match

Below centre The fast bowler's dangerous weapon. Tony Greig ducks under a Wayne Daniel bouncer while Knott looks on

Below right Michael Holding cannot believe his bad luck having just beaten Tony Greig for the fourth time in four balls, and still the England batsman survives

Norman Cowans, England's number one pace man since the retirement of Bob Willis, who is also in the picture

A picture that has become a photographic cliché: Mike Hendrick does leg-stretching exercises with Bernard Thomas, the England physiotherapist, as the television camera records the scene

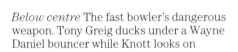

'I did it my way'
Gundappa Viswanath turns his wrists and runs the ball down through the slip area off the face of the bat during the Prudential World Cup match between India and West Indies at Edgbaston, 1979. Variations of this shot have become exceedingly popular in limited-over cricket

Duleep Mendis, the Sri Lankan captain, hits Botham into the Mound Stand at Lord's for one of his three sixes in his innings of 111 and 94 in the Inaugural Test match at Lord's, 1984. Botham bowled several bouncers at Mendis, but the Sri Lankan improvised exciting shots to deal with everything

Below Derek Randall ends up sitting down after hitting a boundary in a John Player League match for Nottinghamshire against Worcestershire at Worcester, 1981. Randall has a style and shot all of his own

Catches at Full Stretch

Allan Lamb takes a superb low catch at third slip to dismiss Joel Garner in the first Test at Edgbaston, 1984, and give Derek Pringle his fifth wicket of the innings. David Gower has moved to the catch as well

Gower is the victim as Allan Border takes a low catch at silly point off the bowling of Ray Bright, Edgbaston, 1981. Marsh is joyful and Gower is out for 23

Below Graham Gooch takes a brilliant one-handed catch low to his left to dismiss Gaekwad off Ian Botham's bowling, England *v* India, Edgbaston, 1979. Hendrick, Miller and Gower complete the slip cordon. Of the three catches pictured on this page, this is the only one where the catcher ended on the winning side

Pitch Invasions

Although the problem has never reached the proportions that it has in soccer, invasions of the pitch by spectators have become all too frequent in recent years. *Above* Rohan Kanhai, the West Indian captain, tries to remove a spectator following an invasion to celebrate Gibbs taking a wicket. Kallicharran, Murray, Foster, umpire Bird, Boyce and Lloyd all give support. The occasion is the Test match at Lord's, 1973. *Left* Clive Lloyd attempts to repel an invasion after Tony Greig has been dismissed at The Oval, 1976

Below A political protest at Lord's in 1984. Tamil demonstrators lie down on the pitch as the England–Sri Lanka inaugural Test match at Lord's is about to start. Stewards remove them as umpires Evans and Bird look anxiously at the wicket and Chris Broad waits

The Indian fans congregate below the Indian dressing-room balcony to show their appreciation while they wait for the Man-of-the-Match presentation to Mohinder Amarnath

The ugly face of the hooligan at international cricket. The Indian supporters celebrate after India has beaten England in the semi-final of the Prudential World Cup at Old Trafford in 1983. It was a joyous occasion and a memorable one in cricket history. This was spoiled by the taint of violence as a group of young English 'fans' (whose hats betray their allegiance to another sport) fists clenched and beer cans in hand, move in to attack the Indian supporters while chanting racist slogans. The police quickly intervened and an ugly scene was avoided, but the threat to cricket as a family game is apparent and it would be well to consider making future presentations and awards in the privacy of the pavilion or dressing room

Mohsin Khan, the Pakistani opening batsman who, in forty Tests, scored 2,468 runs. His most memorable innings was the one in which he is seen here: 200 against England at Lord's

Batting Heroes of the 1970s and 1980s

David Steele, Northamptonshire, Derbyshire and England, was a mid-seventies hero, for he withstood the might of the West Indies to score 106 at Trent Bridge in 1976, having scored fifties in his first three Tests against Lillee and Thomson the previous season. After eight successful Tests in two years he was dropped and never played international cricket again. He was a very useful slow left-arm bowler and he retired from cricket in 1984

Graham Gooch pulls a ball to the boundary. One of the most exciting batsmen England has ever produced, he was banned from Test cricket from 1982 to 1985, but he returned with two centuries and a fifty in three Texaco Trophy games against Australia in 1985. He was the most prolific run scorer in English cricket in the early eighties

Javed Miandad of Pakistan, Sussex and Glamorgan. He hit a double century in a Test match against New Zealand at Karachi in 1976 when he was only 19 years, 141 days old, and by 1985, Javed had passed 5,000 runs in Test cricket and hit thirteen centuries. He was still a few months short of his twenty-eighth birthday

Hilary 'Larry' Gomes who provides the rocklike steadiness to a flamboyant West Indian batting line-up in the eighties. A consistent left-hander, he played for Middlesex before he became a Test cricketer

Alvin Kallicharran, a brilliant left-hander who was banned from Test cricket for his association with South Africa, but not before he had played sixty-six Tests for the West Indies and scored 4,399 runs. He has prospered for Warwickshire and Orange Free State and did captain the West Indies for a while

The Fine Art of Spin
Kerry O'Keeffe, one of the long line of Australian leg-spinners, who took 85 wickets in twenty-four Tests and who played two seasons for Somerset. Characteristic of O'Keeffe was the left arm flung across, but the middle picture of the sequence shows the high action which leads into the full follow-through essential to the successful leg-break and googly bowler

Ease of action is all important to the spinner and the two pictures of Derek Underwood (*below*) show his improvement in the earlier part of his career. In the first picture he is bowling for England in 1970,

but the knee is slightly bent and he appears to be off balance. In the second picture, the Benson and Hedges Final of 1973, he has rectified his fault and the arm is higher. 'Dusty' Rhodes is umpire in both pictures

Norman Gifford, who took more than a hundred wickets in a season for Warwickshire at the age of forty-three, shows determination as he makes the easy leap into his delivery stride

Spin Bowling

Abdul Qadir, the most gifted leg-break and googly bowler and the most successful in Test cricket in recent years. Pakistan teammates have described Qadir as a spin bowler with the temperament and aggression of a fast man. A neat stylist with a quick arm action, he follows through with his right arm going across the body to the left knee. Ken Palmer is the umpire

John Emburey, an off-spin bowler of the highest quality, shows great concentration at the point of delivery

Phil Edmonds delivers with an upright action, but in this picture his concentration appears to be focussed on the ball. He is an intelligent and innovative bowler

Ray Bright, captain of Victoria, was Australia's main spinner for some years, during a time when fast bowlers were very much in the limelight

167

Clive Lloyd

Clive Hubert Lloyd retired from Test cricket in January, 1985, after a career of unparalleled success as captain of the West Indies. He played in 110 Tests and scored 7,515 runs with nineteen centuries. He led his country on seventy-four occasions and suffered defeat only eleven times. He also captained Lancashire and Guyana and as a batsman was dynamic. In 1976 he equalled Gilbert Jessop's record by reaching 200 in 120 minutes. An unlikely looking batsman as he lolloped onto the field wearing his spectacles, his shoulders slightly hunched, he had a feline grace as he batted and fielded which thrilled all who watched him. He led the West Indies to victory in two Prudential World Cups, and to the runners-up position in 1983. His career began in 1963 and he was in the Lancashire side, although he had relinquished the captaincy, in 1985. He has scored more than 30,000 runs in first-class cricket.

The power and beauty of Lloyd's batting can be seen here. With perfect timing and balance he drives Underwood over long-on for six. Alan Knott and Chris Old look on in wonder and admiration

Clive Lloyd spent the earlier part of his career fielding in the covers where his anticipation, speed, pick up and throw caused him to be likened to a cat. In his later years he has specialised in the slips, and his fielding has been as brilliant there as it was in the covers

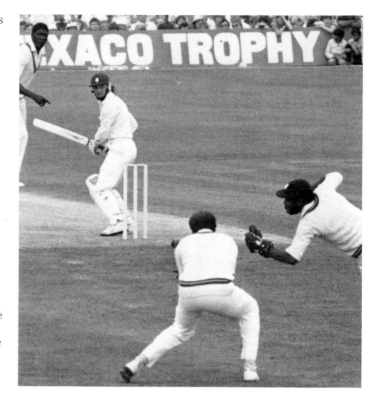

Right In the Texaco Trophy match at Old Trafford in 1984, Graeme Fowler edges a ball from Garner. Dujon dives across towards Lloyd's line of vision and the ball is travelling very quickly; it can be seen by Lloyd's left shoulder. Lloyd holds the catch and falls backward with the impact. As Fowler walks towards the pavilion, Garner applauds. Dujon looks on, bewildered

Below One of the many triumphs enjoyed by the West Indies under Clive Lloyd's captaincy. He holds the 1979 World cup and his team-mates laugh happily. (Left to right) Croft, Richards, Garner, King, Holding, Kallicharran, Lloyd, Deryck Murray and Greenidge

West Indies' Domination
Andy Roberts, the spearhead of the West Indian attack in the 1970s and a very great fast bowler. Here he is bowling at Bob Woolmer at Headingley in 1976. David Constant is the umpire

Centre Jubilation at speed. Holding leaps in appeal and is joined by the slip cordon and wicket-keeper; (left to right) Richards, Greenidge, King and Deryck Murray who has taken the catch to dismiss Alan Ward at Headingley, 1976

Below The pace dominance continues into the next decade: Geoff Miller is caught by Dujon off Holding, Edgbaston, 1984, and again the slips erupt

The end of a very great limited-over match. Deryck Murray (*right*) is mobbed by West Indian supporters after scoring 61 not out and sharing a last wicket partnership with Andy Roberts that brought the West Indies victory by one wicket over Pakistan in the Prudential World Cup at Edgbaston, 1975

Centre The return of the spinner. Roger Harper has David Gower caught behind at Headingley, 1984. The West Indian fielders run to congratulate the tall off-spinner as the umpire's finger goes up

Below The spinner strikes again. A brilliant low catch by Desmond Haynes at forward short-leg gets rid of Ian Botham off Harper's bowling in the second innings of the Old Trafford Test, 1984. Harper took 6 for 57

Viv Richards

Viv Richards is possibly the greatest batsman that cricket has known since Don Bradman. He has now played in eighty-three Test matches, a number surpassed by only two other West Indians, Clive Lloyd and Gary Sobers. He has hit over 6,000 Test runs and more than 25,000 in his career. His powers show no sign of diminishing, for in 1985 he hit a career best 322 for Somerset against Warwickshire at Taunton. In addition to his brilliant batting, he is an exciting fielder and a useful bowler. In the picture (*left*) he has just caught Frank Hayes at slip off the bowling of Andy Roberts. Hayes walks away dejectedly, Roberts raises his arms, King and Greenidge acclaim the catch as Richards, capped as usual, cries out his delight.

Below left Richards in action for West Indies *v* England at The Oval in 1976. He has every shot in his repertoire. He made 291 in this innings which brought his aggregate for the series to 829, a West Indian record. His innings lasted for 472 minutes and he hit thirty-eight fours and faced only 386 deliveries. *Below centre* A cover drive off Greig in the first Test of the same series at Trent Bridge when he hit 232. *Below right* A leg glance in the same innings

Premature jubilation by Richards (*right*) as he celebrates the early dismissal of Gavaskar in the Prudential World Cup Final of 1983. Gavaskar walks away dejectedly, having been caught behind for 2, as Haynes and Richards, arm raised, run to congratulate Roberts, the bowler. India went on to win the match

Below In 1984, the West Indies beat England by five Tests to nil, so inflicting the first whitewash on England in England. Richards began the series with an innings of 117 at Edgbaston. In the picture (*left*), he drives fiercely through the off side. His pleasure at reaching his hundred is plain to see. He lifts his bat to acknowledge the applause of the crowd and a fellow West Indian runs on to give his personal congratulations

Ian Botham

In 1973, a burly young man made his debut for Somerset in a John Player League match. The following season he blossomed as a fast-medium paced bowler and as a batsman of ferocious power. In 1977, at the age of twenty-one, he was in the England side. His name was Ian Terence Botham, now established as one of the greatest, possibly *the* greatest, all-rounders in cricket history.

Botham displays the power of his off-drive during his first innings for England

Below Botham's Test debut came at Trent Bridge. By mid-afternoon Australia were 131 for 2 and he was brought back for his second spell. His first ball was short and Greg Chappell, intending a drive, edged the ball into his stumps. Chappell looks stunned. Botham raises his arms in triumph at his first Test wicket. In the space of thirty-four deliveries Botham took 4 for 13, including Rod Marsh (*below right*) lbw for 0 as Brearley and Greig smile. He finished with 5 for 74 and the most remarkable Test career of recent years had begun

At international level over the next seven years the extrovert 'Bionic Botham' took wickets with astounding frequency and tasted constant success

Below Bob Willis feeds Botham with champagne after the memorable victory at Edgbaston in 1981, when Botham took 5 for 11 to give England a win over Australia by 29 runs. Botham, not for the only time in that remarkable series, was named Man-of-the-Match. He holds his cheque in his left hand and the medal in his right. He hit two thrilling hundreds, at Leeds and Manchester, which turned the course of each match and took 34 wickets in the series, and this after resigning the captaincy at the end of the second Test at Lord's

Below right Anderson of New Zealand is lbw to Botham for 19 and his disconsolate look contrasts with the smiles of Brearley, the England captain, and of Botham himself

Even the 'Bionic Botham' is troubled by injury, although he makes little of it; he arrived with his arm in a sling for the meeting at Lord's in October, 1978, when the team was issued with kit, but he played throughout the tour of Australia which followed. Never resting from sport, he plays table 'Test Match Game' with skipper Bob Willis

Below In March, 1984, he is in bed following a knee operation at Woodlands Hospital, Birmingham, after his return from Pakistan. Botham, surrounded by all the modern comforts, takes a call from a well-wisher

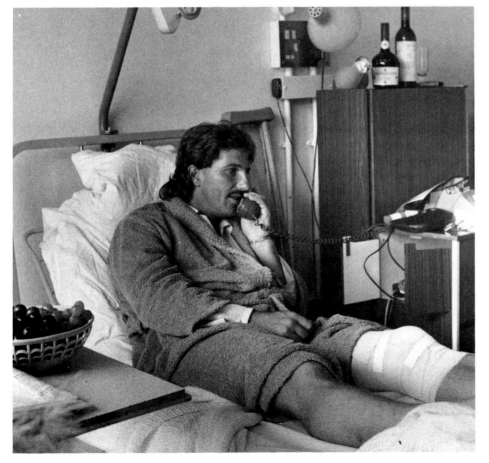

Opposite Botham proves that he is human and capable of error. In the Benson and Hedges Quarter Final, Somerset *v* Warwickshire at Edgbaston, 1984, he survives an appeal for lbw by Willis. The *Comedy of Errors* begins as Botham, Willis and non-striking batsman Trevor Gard all look at umpire Ray Julien, who ignores the appeal. Meanwhile, the ball goes through to wicket-keeper Geoff Humpage.

Humpage has spotted Botham moving down the wicket and runs towards the stumps, clutching the ball. Botham sees the danger, but Gard is still looking at the umpire.

Realising that he will be run out, Botham calls to Gard to run, but the reaction has come too late; Botham is stranded, and Somerset go out of the Benson and Hedges Cup

To a batsman of his ability, temperament and panache, reputations are meaningless. In this picture he drives Dennis Lillee, the great Australian Test bowler, back over his head for 6 during his innings of 118 at Old Trafford in 1981. He hit 6 sixes in the innings

Below left Ian Botham remains undaunted and unrestrained by occasion. He hooks Holding into the crowd during the 1984 England-West Indies series

He drives majestically through the covers off Malcolm Marshall at Lord's, 1984, and reaches 4,000 runs in Test cricket

The Oval, 1984; Greenidge is lbw to a ball that comes back sharply. It is Botham's 298th Test wicket

A few moments later Jeffrey Dujon became Botham's 300th Test victim when he could only touch a steeply rising delivery to Tavaré at slip, who holds the ball high above his head as the bowler leaps in triumph. Wicket-keeper Paul Downton looks on. Botham became the fifth bowler to achieve 300 Test wickets; the other four are Trueman, Gibbs, Lillee and Willis

The great Viv Richards is tempted to destruction with a bouncer which he hooks into the hands of Paul Allott at long leg. Botham has taken 299 Test wickets

A Season of Spills and Bumps

In the 1984 Test series between England and the West Indies, two English batsmen suffered serious injury. The pictures (*left*) show Andy Lloyd of Warwickshire struck on the temple by a ball from Malcolm Marshall. At the top, Lloyd falls to the ground and holds his temple. In the lower picture he indicates to his captain David Gower and to physiotherapist Bernard Thomas that his vision is impaired. It was Lloyd's Test debut. He did not play again during the season.

In the pictures below, Paul Terry is shown in the Test match at Old Trafford. His arm has been broken, but he returns at the end of the England innings, the injured arm in a sling under his sweater. Garner produces the perfect yorker which thankfully ends his ordeal.

When wicket-keepers collide. Opposing wicket-keepers Bairstow (the batsman) and Dujon are in collision in the Texaco Trophy match at Lord's in 1984. Bairstow has gone for a short run and Dujon has attempted to run him out

Malcolm Marshall returns to the fray at Headingley in 1984 and bats one-handed to give Larry Gomes the chance to reach his century. A damaged wrist is heavily bandaged and Marshall manages to hit a four one-handed. Then he took 7 for 53 and bowled the West Indies to success

England, 1984–5
Graeme Fowler, an enterprising opening batsman, who hit 201 against India at Madras and scored runs briskly in Test cricket even though his technique never satisfied the critics.

Below left Mike Gatting could not reproduce at international level the consistent form that he had shown at county level. A fine striker of the ball, he was appointed vice-captain for the tour to India, and responded with his maiden Test hundred in his thirty-first Test; he followed this with 207 at Madras and topped the England averages at 95.83 for the series. *Below* Allan Lamb, the Northamptonshire batsman who was born in South Africa but qualified to play for England, took three Test hundreds off the West Indies in 1984 and a fourth Test hundred later in the summer off the Sri Lankan bowlers

Australia, 1984–5

Allan Border, an inspiring leader of the Australian side to England in 1985. He began the tour with a record four centuries in his first four first-class innings and was Australia's man-of-the-series in the Texaco Trophy. This picture was taken during his innings of 85 at Edgbaston.

Below left Craig McDermott, the Queensland fast bowler, was the youngest player to appear for Australia for twenty years when he made his debut against the West Indies. *Below centre* Dirk Wellham, who won his place in the side after leading New South Wales to victory in the Sheffield Shield and McDonald's Cup and batting splendidly throughout the Australian season. *Below right* Andrew Hilditch, opening batsman and vice-captain, who scored a century in the first Test at Headingley

David Gower

In 1984, David Gower was appointed captain of England. A left-handed batsman of great charm with 4,653 runs in seventy Tests to his credit, Gower could not have had a more difficult apprenticeship in the position as the England team, bereft of some of its leading players because of the ban imposed after it had played in South Africa, was routed by the West Indies. Gower led the England party to India in the winter of 1984–5, and once again was confronted with the hardest of tasks. Following the assassination of Mrs Ghandi, the Indian Prime Minister, the tragedy of Bhopal and the murder of the British Deputy High Commissioner to Western India, the tour was initially in doubt, and a saddened England side were beaten in the first Test, but Gower rallied his side, instilled fine team spirit and became only the fourth English captain in Test history to win a rubber abroad after coming from behind.

In the Lord's Test of 1984, he directs operations for Geoff Miller while Derek Pringle ponders and umpire David Evans organises the sightscreen. The problem that confronted Gower was how to contain Gordon Greenidge, who stands by umpire Evans. Greenidge scored 214 not out in the second innings to give West Indies an historic victory

Below left Gower pulls a ball to the boundary during his highest Test innings, 200 not out *v* India, Edgbaston, 1979. Reddy is the wicket-keeper. *Below right* He takes a sharp slip catch to dismiss John Wright of New Zealand at The Oval, 1983. Edmonds runs to congratulate him

The Illustration of Cricket and the Evolution of Cricket Photography
An interview with Ken Kelly

Cricket is a subject which has always excited the artist, encapsulating for many, as it does, an English way of life and a code of conduct. Francis Hayman, RA, painted the game of cricket as played on the Artillery Ground, London, in 1743, and he was by no means the first artist to be attracted to the game.

Over the next 150 years, as the popularity of cricket grew, so did the interest of artists. Some of the leading illustrators of the day, like George Frederick Watts who was born in 1817 and admitted to the Royal Academy at the age of eighteen, were excited by the gesture and movement of the game. Watts was befriended by Nicholas Felix, a fine cricketer, who commissioned him to make some drawings from life of some of the batting strokes. In 1837, a series of these in the form of lithographs was published and 'had only to be seen to be coveted by every cricket player'. It was Watts who provided most of the famous illustrations to *Felix on the Bat*: 'Play!,' 'Forward', 'Leg Volley', 'The Draw', 'The Cut', and, for the second edition, 'The Catapulta'. Felix himself was also an artist and drew several of the famous players of the time, such as William Clarke and Thomas Box.

In 1868 *Vanity Fair*, for forty-six years the most discussed and successful magazine of the age, was first published, and in 1877 it issued its first cricket cartoon, a drawing by Spy entitled 'Cricket' in the *Men of Our Day* series. Cricket was, of course, Dr W. G. Grace. Nearly fifty cricketers were featured in cartoons over the next thirty-seven years, mostly by Spy, Sir Leslie Ward, and Ape, Carlo Pellegrini.

Equally coveted by collectors of cricket memorabilia are the forty-eight plates portraying 'characteristic attitudes of famous players executed in crayon' by Albert Chevallier Tayler, which were issued in 1905.

By this time, however, cricket photography had come into being, and the art of the photographer was to revolutionise the recording of cricketers and cricket history, as it had revolutionised the technique of artists in the latter part of the nineteenth century. This book illustrates the art of cricket photography, an art that is more than a hundred years old, and one which the artist featured in this book, Ken Kelly, has practised for nearly half a century.

There is much speculation, and little evidence, as to who took the earliest cricket photographs. Of the technique, however, we can be certain.

The shutter exposure in the earliest days of photography was measured in minutes, and, even in the latter part of the nineteenth century, it was often measured in seconds. This meant that most photographs had to be portraits and family groups, and cricket photographs fell into the same category, with poses of batting stance or bowling action. In the latter part of the century there was a development in that photographers began to take action pictures, not during matches, but in practice areas where they set up stumps and encouraged bowlers and batsmen to go through their paces to a set pattern. The photographer would use his large studio camera, with glass plates varying from 8″ × 6″ to 12″ × 10″ in size, to record action shots of the famous players of the day, many of whom were national heroes.

In 1851, Frederick Scott Archer had invented the wet collodion process which enabled photographers to make their own plates without patent restrictions, and allowed them to experiment with photographic emulsions. Lenses with larger apertures were being developed, as were faster shutter speeds which would eventually lead to successful action photography.

Cricket had gained immense popularity, almost entirely due to the dominant personality of W. G. Grace and the standing which he had attained throughout the country and the empire. Inevitably, popularity leads to some kind of commercial involvement and, for the cricket photographer, this came with the advent of postcards.

It was Emmanuel Herman who suggested to the British postal authorities that people should be allowed to send a piece of light card with limited space for writing through the post at a reduced cost. This practice was introduced to England in 1870, and in 1894 the Post Office allowed commercially printed pictorial postcards to be sent through the post. These early postcards had to have the reverse side kept free for the address, so that any message had to be written on the illustrated side, but in 1902 the printers were permitted to split the reverse side of the card into two, one half for the correspondence and the other for the address. So the present-day postcard started, and the photographers of the day were kept busy. Over 500 million cards were sent in 1900 alone.

The popularity of both the postcard and of cricket encouraged photographers to take pictures of cricketers for use on this new form of correspondence. Thus the first cricket photographers were stimulated in their work by the prospect of commercial success. Another development was the use of photographs in books on the game, which were becoming more popular.

Chaffin, Gillman, Stearn, Russell, Winter, Hawkins & Co and W. A. Rouch were among the earlier photographers, and the most prolific seems to have been Hawkins & Co, although W. A. Rouch produced many memorable photographs for C. B. Fry's *The Book of Cricket* (1899) and for other books of the period.

At the turn of the century George Beldam, who played for Middlesex and for W. G. Grace's London County side, and who hit nine first-class hundreds, began to take photographs, no doubt learning much from watching other professional photographers at work. His intimate knowledge of the game and his friendship with many players gave him a distinct advantage. He produced a number of fine action shots and also his own books, notably *Great Batsmen, Their Methods at a Glance* (1907). Beldam was able to benefit from the pioneering work and the innovations of the earlier photographers; one must not forget their work and give credit to Beldam alone as so often, wrongly, happens. He was one of the last, and probably the most distinguished, photographers to use the studio camera to take action pictures of noted players, and his skill in capturing the action was extraordinary.

From the turn of the century, photographers were trying to take action shots at matches, using short focal length telephoto lenses. They were long-distance shots showing play in progress but they did capture the atmosphere, characters and conditions of the time. These pictures, and the action shots taken in practice areas, took cricket photography up to World War I.

The war brought about a revolution in cricket photography, for lenses made for aerial reconnaissance were adapted for photographing cricket. The initial problem for the photographer was how to obtain one of these lenses, which were mostly German: Zeiss or Dallmeyer. They were prized possessions and were of 20″, 30″, 40″, 50″ or, like the one at Central Press, 48″ focal length. These lenses led to the development of the 'Long Tom' camera, which consisted of the lens, the housing for the lens, and the camera fitted onto the other end of the housing. It was the standard camera until the late 1960s, and some remained in use in the 1970s.

The format of the camera used on the 'Long Toms' changed over the years. In the early days they usually had a half-plate reflex camera, which allowed the camera to be focussed after each over on near or far wicket, or anywhere on the ground at a given time. However, this was a lengthy business. The half-plate format meant that the area covered was quite large, including the batsman and slips, but the batsman could be enlarged from the central area if so desired. A wicket could, however, be missed if the photographer was concentrating on a bowling picture, for then the sheath had to be put back into the plate slide, taken out of the camera, another slide put into the camera and the sheath taken out again. This was quite time-consuming and, if a spin bowler was on, one or two balls could be missed.

Ken Kelly photographed in 1939

The 'Long Tom' was from 4 to 6 feet in length, had brass or metal fittings, and was very heavy, and therefore static; once in position it was there for the day. It was often designed and made by the photographer, or by an engineer or craftsman-carpenter in conjunction with the photographer, and it was always made with loving care and regarded with affection.

Glass plates were used and housed in protective casings, single metal or double dark slides. These were large and heavy and usually only twelve or eighteen plates could be taken to each assignment. If the plates were sent back to the newspaper or agency, they were sometimes reloaded and returned, especially during Test matches, but generally the twelve or eighteen slides would have to suffice for the day. When one considers that with these the photographer would have to cover wickets, batting and bowling pictures, and other incidents, the expertise needed becomes obvious.

The 'Long Tom' was usually stationed in an elevated

position at long-on, or directly above the wicket, so that the batsman was in the picture with the slip fielders also in view. It was so heavy that a tripod was not often used, but beer crates were borrowed to support the back while the front was rested on a balcony, and a chock of wood was used to lift the back of the camera for photographing the near wicket and pulling back for the far wicket. It may have been unsophisticated, but the results show how effective it was.

The photographers' knowledge of the game, their skill and anticipation and their ability to press the shutter release at the right moment was the art of cricket photography: one opportunity, one picture. Today, a photographer has 36-exposure film and a motor-wind, but he rarely gets any better pictures of wickets. In fact, pictures of wickets are rarely used by newspapers today. More popular are the 'after the action' shots of bowlers running down the wicket, arms in the air, or of players slapping hands and hugging one another.

All the national newspapers had 'Long Tom' cameras, but these were mostly used for general news, such as picturing the Royal Family on the balcony at Buckingham Palace, and for sporting events. Most of the big agencies had 'Long Toms', and some were used in provincial cities, usually those that were Test match venues. In all only about thirty of these cameras were to be found in England. There were a few in Australia and South Africa, reputedly one in New Zealand, but probably only about thirty-eight in the cricket-playing world. Two of the main agencies, Sport and General and Central Press, owned four to six each, so that only about twenty 'Long Toms' were used regularly for cricket.

The London newspapers used pictures from the two main agencies who had sole rights at the two London Test grounds: Central Press at The Oval, Sport and General at Lord's. Until 1972 these two agencies had national and international rights for immediate picture release at all Test grounds. Local newspapers in Manchester, Leeds, Nottingham and Birmingham could take pictures for immediate local use and for publication in books at a later date. It was this concession that enabled Kelly to cover Tests in Leeds and Birmingham and to complete his hundredth Test match coverage at Trent Bridge in 1983, having begun at Leeds in 1938. Now, if he covers tours abroad, a cricket photographer can cover a hundred Tests in ten to twelve years, but Kelly's career had started with the *Yorkshire Evening News*' 'Long Tom', with its 40″ Dallmeyer lens, located on the balcony at Headingley in 1938.

After World War II more lenses came onto the market. The British lenses came from the F-24 RAF camera, the most popular being the 36″ Ross lens, and a 50″ Ross which was developed after the war. The 36″ lens could be bought from service-surplus shops for between £30 and £50, but the complete 'Long Tom'

The four 'Long Toms' on the balcony of the Headingley pavilion at the side of the press box. One more camera was situated above the wicket and this was the largest number of cameras seen on a Test ground

cost considerably more. More German lenses became available, but, as these were often snapped up by bird and wildlife photographers, they too became scarce.

As the agencies still retained the rights to Test grounds and thus a virtual monopoly of cricket photography, few freelancers owned 'Long Tom' cameras. Kelly was an exception. He had one in the mid-fifties, as did Bob Trasler of Park Pictures and Geoff Hallawell in Manchester, but, as there was little money to be made, very few other freelancers were in their position. The scene is very different today when photographers, some more experienced than others, crowd into grounds.

Leeds was a great centre of both cricket and cricket photography, with Kelly's close friends Jack Hickes of the *Yorkshire Evening News* and Harry Fletcher of the *Yorkshire Evening Post* in the forefront. Other photographers from Yorkshire papers were Frank Carlill, Fred Dale, Jack Tordoff, Irving Crawford, Dennis Richmond and Johnny Muscroft, among others. Sheffield and Bradford newspapers also owned 'Long Toms', so that there were always colleagues and friendly rivals in attendance on Yorkshire grounds.

In 1947 the old 40″ 'Long Tom' Dallmeyer was re-designed and made smaller by a firm named Culkins, under the direction of Ronnie Newbold. To make the 'Long Tom' smaller usually meant fixing a 9cm × 12cm camera on the back. A 5″ × 4″ camera could also be utilised, and the *Yorkshire Post* used a 5½″ × 3½″ postcard-size camera. The disadvantages of the new design was that, as there was no reflex housing on the camera, the photographer had to focus in the morning on a ground-glass focussing screen, and mark the spot

carrying handles, and it was extremely heavy, although it only had a 36″ Ross lens. It had, in fact, been made by a firm who were used by undertakers.

Leslie Deakins, the Warwickshire secretary, designated a position at the right-hand side of the balcony where it was to be placed. There were steep steps up to the balcony which changed direction in the middle. The 'Long Tom' had to be driven to the ground in a van – it was too big for a car – and Kelly and the driver took nearly half an hour to negotiate the steps to the balcony and get the 'Long Tom' in place. The members on the balcony doffed their hats to the 'coffin' as it passed and hummed the funeral march. They had a sense of humour which was, and still is, appreciated by

Len Hutton walks out to bat during the 1953 Test trial at Edgbaston. Above his head in the background can be seen the photographers' box, the first of its kind. This was the box that Kelly used to work from

Two Yorkshire Evening News photographers pictured at Headingley in 1946: Jack Hickes working the camera with Kelly waiting to take over

The same photographers, pictured in 1985, with the same 'Long Tom'

for the far and near wicket. He had to be very accurate because, if he had to focus again, he had to take the glass-plate slide out of the camera to do it. If an incident occurred outside the focus of the two wickets, he could not take a quick picture. Many of the agencies kept the old reflex cameras.

When Kelly moved to Birmingham in 1948 the Birmingham Gazette and Despatch Group had the first 'Long Tom' to be used by a newspaper in that city. He did not see it until after his appointment and shortly before the start of the season. It was 6 feet long, made of ¾ inch mahogany, had brass fittings including

Kelly. The incident formed a bond with the members which has continued to the present day.

The early years at Edgbaston were most happy and a fine relationship was forged between players, press and photographer. On one occasion Charles Harrold, a Birmingham sports writer and broadcaster, was talking about Eric Hollies' mannerisms as he ran up to bowl. He and Kelly wanted pictures of Hollies in action to support the article that was being done for the *Sports Argus*, but Hollies was bowling at the City End and they needed him at the Pavilion End if Kelly was to picture him with the 'Long Tom'. They lunched with the players and told skipper 'Tom' Dollery of their problem. Dollery said he was trying to win the match, but he agreed to give Hollies three overs from the Pavilion End straight after lunch to give Kelly time to get his pictures.

Dollery kept his word and Hollies took two wickets. Kelly had got his pictures, but Dollery kept Hollies at the Pavilion End where he took three more wickets, so the skipper thanked Kelly and Harrold for their advice. Hollies told Kelly that if they won the championship that season, he would appear in the team photograph instead of taking it. Unfortunately the team did not win the championship.

In 1949, the large 'Long Tom' was changed, and the housing was made smaller. This 'Long Tom' was the work of fellow-photographer Bob Trasler, who took it with him when he moved to Manchester in 1952. The third 'Long Tom' was made by photographer Ray Hayward, and this was the best of the three. He used a 36″ Ross lens with a 9cm × 12cm V/N camera on the back. It was small, neat and well made, and Kelly used it to take many of the pictures in this book.

When he became freelance in 1956 he used another 'Long Tom' that was made for him by Hayward. As Hayward also made one for the *Oxford Mail*, he made three in all and Kelly cherishes his to this day.

Kelly's move from Birmingham is related earlier in this book, as is his return and the change from 'Long Tom' to 35mm equipment. His return to Birmingham in 1967 was due to photographer Alan Hill of the *Birmingham Post and Mail*, and to Frank Carlill whom Kelly had known in Leeds since 1939. Carlill had become picture editor of the *Birmingham Post* in 1967, and his admiration for Ken Kelly as friend and photographer meant that he asked him to cover cricket for the paper as a freelancer until 1981.

We have heard how Kelly bought a 35mm camera, a 400mm lens and a 2X converter in Japan and used them first in Australia. From 1968 he used this more sophisticated equipment on a full-time basis. For the Edgbaston Test in 1968 he bought two more cameras and a 600mm lens so that he could give full cricket coverage for any eventuality: the 600mm lens for the close-ups of batting and bowling action, and the 300mm and 400mm lenses for incidents such as the fall of wickets and slip catches.

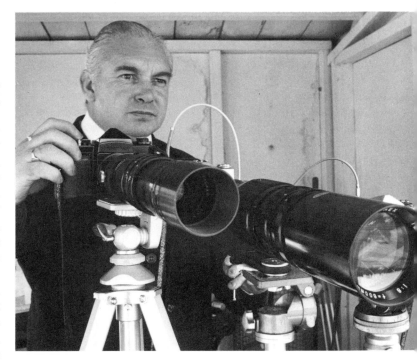

Kelly with a battery of three cameras and lenses: on the left is a 300mm lens, next to it a 600mm lens, and on the right, partially covered, a 200mm lens. The picture was taken at Edgbaston, 1970

The problem now arose that when a 300mm or 400mm lens was on the tripod, something might happen which demanded a close-up shot; the reverse could occur when the 600mm was mounted. In the past photographers had bolted two cameras together by the two tripod bushes, especially when covering horse-racing. This enabled them to take a picture of the horses coming over the fence with the top camera and to keep the bottom camera free to use if a horse fell. Kelly adopted a similar system, using three lenses, each mounted on its own tripod and worked by antinous releases. Two were strapped together to work from one hand while the third was worked by the other hand. It demanded much concentration, but it worked and very little was missed within the range of the lenses so that any type of picture could be taken.

This was devised and used in 1969, and Kelly appeared in the press and was featured on a lens advertisement. Others followed the practice and one photographer, Patrick Eagar, devised a bar to put on the tripod, which meant that two lenses could be used on the same tripod. Later, he began to use a remote-control camera mounted some 40 to 70 yards away in another part of the ground, which was operated from the central release where he worked with his other cameras.

In the late 1960s Kelly, Eagar, Jack Hickes and his son David, from Leeds, and Geoff Hallawell of Manchester were the only freelancers to cover cricket regularly. The two main agencies still dominated the Test scene and they and other agencies covered a few county games, but it was not until 1972 that the

Geoff Hallawell with the 48″ 'Long Tom' that he used at Old Trafford

growth in cricket photography, and in the number of photographers, really began. Test matches were opened up to national newspapers, other agencies and the established freelance. Now, coverage is even more open at all grounds except Lord's, which is still subject to certain restrictions.

Colour photography was experimented with successfully by two freelancers, Kelly and Eagar, as well as by a couple of agencies, and a few newspaper and magazine photographers, although the emulsion speed of the film was not as it is today. There is an early colour photograph of Don Bradman, taken by Sport and General in 1948, and Kelly took a colour transparency of Mike Smith in 1959, but these were posed, not action, pictures. As the only lenses available at the time were F/5.6 or F/8, colour photographs could only be taken in good light. Today colour photography is as common as black-and-white, and with telephoto lenses with apertures of F/2.8, F/3.5 and F/4 and colour emulsion speeds of 100 to 400 ASA, it presents few problems.

The developments in lens manufacture over the last fifteen to twenty-five years have been quite outstanding. Leading Japanese companies like Nikon and Canon have made sports photography, technically, a relatively simple art, and there have been some dramatic changes. One of the modern innovations has been the motor-wind, which allows a certain number of frames per second to be taken in sequence. Sadly, it has become much overused, but utilised properly it means that very little of any incident that takes place within the range of the lens need be missed. Kelly did not use a motor-wind until 1975, although they had been in production for twenty years by then. He felt that it would upset his acute timing of the shutter release; even now he believes that the first picture he takes is the one he would have taken in the past, but he keeps the motor-wind running in certain circumstances so that he can record the action subsequent to the main picture, or for bowling sequences. Automatic exposure systems have also helped the photographer.

The telephoto lenses in use at present are masterpieces of optical skill and precision engineering. A 600mm F/4 lens can cost more than £3,000. The brilliant new teleconverters, which can cost up to £300 increase the focal length of a lens, thus giving the photographer many more options. The optical quality means sharper pictures with good contrast and high definition. Cameras change year by year, and automatic focussing is available at a price, but it all enables the photographer to concentrate more on the picture and less on the camera.

Even so, the top cricket photographers have to give six hours of deep concentration in a day's cricket, which can be just as mentally exhausting as batting or slip fielding. A knowledge of the game remains essential if a photographer is to really understand what is going on.

Many photographers have been involved in the development of cricket photography, and Ken Kelly would like to record some of them here.

Central Press

Jimmy Sime, who served with the RFC in World War I, was one of the early photographers of the inter-war years. He was followed by George Frankland, Dennis Oulds, Len Burt, Terry Disney and Jack Wright, all of whom had experience of working at Test matches.

George Frankland was, for many, the father of cricket photography. He was with the Central News Agency until 1934 when he moved to Central Press. He

George Frankland, with colleague Johnny Horton, look at a cricket negative in the Press Association darkrooms

moved to the Press Association after World War II and covered cricket for them into the 1960s.

Bob Stiggins joined Central Press shortly before World War II, and later moved to the *News Chronicle* and then the *Daily Express*. He still covers cricket.

Dennis Oulds was the doyen of cricket photographers after World War II. He was with Central Press from 1935 until his retirement in 1981.

Central Press eventually had six 'Long Toms', with a 50″, 48″, 40″, 36″, 20″ and a 30″ lens that was from a studio camera and was used from a position directly above the wicket. It was an extraordinary lens that seemed to be sharp on both wickets and to the boundary beyond.

Sport and General Agency

Bill Bishop, Jack Fletcher, Leslie Davies (who was killed in World War II), Mark Seymour, Ken Saunders, Vic Fowler and Brian Thomas all covered Tests. This agency had four 'Long Toms', with 50″, 40″, 36″ and 28″ lenses.

Many of these photographers worked outside cricket as well, and Bert Mason of the *Daily Mail* took the famous picture of St Paul's in the midst of the blitz, from the roof of the *Daily Mail* building.

Leslie Priest and Lol Harris were with Associated Press, and, as well as the Leeds photographers already mentioned, there were also Jimmy Waite, a freelancer, and Gordon Priestley of the Bradford *Telegraph and Argus*.

Like Ken Kelly, Bob Stiggins, Dennis Oulds, Jack Hickes and Eric Piper of the *Daily Mirror* (formerly of the John Topham agency) Geoff Hallawell has covered cricket with both 'Long Tom' and 35mm equipment, operating mainly in Manchester since the 1940s. Hallawell also used to photograph Campbell's world-record runs on Coniston Water. He used a Carl Zeiss Triplet lens F/7 with a Shew Reflecta, string blind camera. More recently have come Patrick Eagar, Adrian Murrell and, of late, Graham Morris.

In Australia there has been the legendary Herbert Fishwick who was born in Devon, but who became the father of cricket photography in Australia using a 'Long Tom' with a 48″ lens. Harry Martin did good work for the *Sydney Morning Herald* with the 'Long Tom', and more recently Bruce Postle won a good reputation with the *Melbourne Age*. Viv Jenkins and Philip Tyson, son of the old England fast bowler, represent the modern generation and maintain fine traditions.

The 'Long Tom' is placed precariously on the end of the roof, and Dennis Oulds has come down the catwalk to lower his photographic plates in a sack to a messenger below

Oulds leaving the Oval with the 48″ 'Long Tom', having used it for the last time before retiring in 1981

Brian Thomas with the 50″ 'Long Tom' working from Q Stand at Lord's. The wooden frame of the camera allowed the photographs to be taken well above the members' heads, but it meant that Thomas had to stand on a chair for six hours of play

Watch the birdie! Brian Thomas of Sport and General Agency with the pigeon that settled on his 'Long Tom' to watch the 1957 Test at Headingley

Kelly surrounded by champagne whilst covering his hundredth Test match at Trent Bridge in 1981

Present-day photographers working from the Mound Stand scoreboard at Lord's cricket ground